Aging In Suburbia

*The Must-Have Conversation
About Homes and Driving*

By Jane Gould

For more information and
to contact the author:

www.aginginsuburbia.com
jane@aginginsuburbia.com

Cover Design by Coralee Lazebnikova
First published, September 2014
as Aging (well) in Suburbia, ISBN:
ISBN: 978-0-9908196-0-8

TABLE OF CONTENTS

INTRODUCTION 1

CHAPTER ONE: GROWING UP WITH THE CAR 13

Problems of Aging in Place 19

Who Wants Old Homes? 24

The Financial Wake-Up Call 27

Demographics at the Source 33

Gray Homes Meet Modern Demographics 38

Are Gray Homes "The Right Stuff?" 43

CHAPTER TWO: DRIVE TILL YOU QUALIFY 47

The Boomers Build a Nest Egg 47

Buying Homes and Buying a Lot More 50

Locked into Suburbia 56

Locked into Lifestyle 60

CHAPTER THREE: TRANSPORTATION: "THE KEY"

PROBLEM FOR BOOMERS 67

Drive, Boomer, Drive! 71

Locked into Cars 72

What Drives the Future? 75

Safety of Older Drivers 77

Depending on Public Transit 80

Home Based Services 82

Rethinking Mobility, I 84

Rethinking Mobility, II 87

Debunking the Drive Till You Qualify 90

CHAPTER FOUR: ALL LINKED UP:

TRANSPORTATION, HOMES, & ENVIRONMENT .. 95

Energy Dependent, by Geography 100

Greener Boomers? 102

CHAPTER FIVE: GRAY HOUSE: BOOMER CASH

OUT? 107

Stay-at-Home Financing: Reverse Mortgages 112

Reverse Mortgages Blow Up, Like Balloons 116

Reverse Mortgage as Investment Strategy 118

The Other Alternative: Selling the House 120

Suburban Homes at Policy Crossroads 124

CHAPTER FIVE—PART II: THE COST OF MOVING

ON 129

CHAPTER SIX: GRAY HOMES: SHRINKING THE

KIDS 139

Children at the Center 142

Failure to Launch 147

Rebranding Children and Community 153

CHAPTER SEVEN: THE GAME CHANGER—

BOOMERS AND TECHNOLOGY 157

The Internet: The Death of Distance 168

The Internet: The Death of "Things" Material 173

Is It Simple? 184

Smartphones Reshape Everyday Habits and Habitats 185

Bytes for Bites 187

Unlikely Companions 192

The Home Is Homely.. 193

**CHAPTER EIGHT: CONCLUSIONS AND
RECOMMENDATIONS... 199**

Action Item I: Take Stock of What Is Important 203

Action Item II: Review the Options and Study the Fine
Print 205

Action Item IIa— A Subset for Women......................... 209

Action Item III: Come up with an Alternative
Transportation Plan.. 210

Action Item IV: Keep Active and Involved with
Technology.. 214

Action Item V: Age with Community First (Robots
Second) 217

ACKNOWLEDGEMENTS 221

INDEX.. 223

REFERENCES 229

ABOUT THE AUTHOR 259

INTRODUCTION

The Baby Boom generation, born between 1946 and 1964, have invented many things we take for granted today: the minivan and sports utility vehicle, the ATM machine, personal computers, and the Internet have all been their inspiration. However, it may be in real estate and transportation that the Boomers have left their biggest mark. The far-flung suburbs, McMansions, and two-car families are all Boomer inspired. But very soon, this generation will need to rethink the value of owning their big suburban homes, and driving almost everywhere.

Their next "reinvention" is called retirement. Baby Boomers will have the daunting task of rearranging the pieces that will make up their retirement years. If they can refill the ATM machine, update their computer skills, and make the SUV safer to drive at night, they may achieve some success. But, the biggest problem and the hardest one to tackle will be 'home sweet home.'

One of the few things we do not routinely reinvent as we age are the homes we live in. In fact, more than 50% of the U.S. population have been in their current homes 10 to 19 years, and 27% have been there 20 years or longer. We may clean out our homes and enhance them with safety features but we stay put. This longevity stands in sharp contrast to the busy lives of Baby Boomers, who are accustomed to continual change and renewal.

This book shakes up this convention and argues that Boomers will also need to reinvent their homes if they are going to age-in-place. Unlike their parents' generation, the Baby Boomers were the first generation to have moved to homes in far-flung suburbs. These suburbs suited younger families, but have critical drawbacks for those who wish to age-in-place. Suburbs are remote when you do not drive *well*, and inhospitable when you do not drive *at all*. Most suburban homes have no access to public transportation, walkable streets, or even taxi service. Moreover, suburban homes, many built thirty or forty years ago, are not energy efficient and require extensive upkeep and maintenance. These household issues do not suit an older, aging population. The Baby Boomers, who now range between ages 51 to 69, have begun to retire. Most of them have not considered, at a personal level, what they will do when their homes are too large, their incomes shrink, and their mobility needs are in flux.

On a larger level, we, as a society, have also not come to grips with the impact of this mass retirement on real-estate markets and the broader economy. The Boomers and older age groups own nearly 60 percent of the owner-occupied homes in this country, although these elders represent only one-third of the population. What will happen to real-estate markets as they begin to unload their old, tired, "gray" homes?

There has never been a more opportune time to rethink the nature of our housing stock. The recent housing meltdown has given people pause; it created a reset button on what it means to own a home, and whether it is an appropriate aspiration. In our flexible, agile society, younger people are questioning if it is desirable to be wedded to a single property with a thirty-year mortgage. Many of them view renting, or multi-generational households, as more suitable living arrangements, at least for the short term. Younger people are not alone. Baby Boomers, facing retirement, will also need to confront whether home ownership is appropriate for their needs. Might they find renting, or the multi-generational household, or locating near an urban "village" to be more suitable?

Many Boomers implicitly know that as they reach age seventy or eighty, their large homes could become liabilities, but they are reluctant to deal with this issue head-on. They have also not come to grips with the fact that older women outlive men, so in many ways the coming crisis is bounded by gender. Will older women, first divorced and now widowed, want to undertake the extensive maintenance and repairs for these homes? Will they be able to afford the escalating insurance bills and property taxes?

Today, 14 percent of the U.S. population is age

sixty-five or older, but in fifteen years that number will reach 20 percent. Imagine a country where every fifth person you meet has reached this milestone. Instead of traveling, or spending more time with friends, these seniors will, depending on the time of year, be attempting to cut the grass or shovel snow. Since nearly three-quarters live in car-dependent suburbs, they will also need to find ways to maintain their mobility or stay indoors the rest of the time.

For Baby Boomers, this real-estate conundrum could not have come at a worse time. Until recently, this was a generation graced with financial largesse. Boomers went through school without accumulating much debt. For twenty or more years, they held relatively secure jobs. Many inherited bank accounts from their thrifty parents. Today, all of this is unraveling. Boomers need a "nest egg" to finance their retirement needs and ever increasing health care costs as their jobs have disappeared. The Great Recession hit just as Boomers were reaching their peak salary years and many will never return to the labor market. Meanwhile, their children and grandchildren have extended their educations with mountains of debt that makes them less willing, and less able, to qualify as first-time home buyers. The implications are immense, both at the personal level, and for the larger economy.

The financial setbacks are only part of the story though. Many would argue that the most daunting reason to "reinvent" homes has to do with transportation. The Baby Boomers are known as the sprawl generation. They are the first generation to embrace the two-car family, and develop a life-style based fully around cars. In their eagerness to become house owners, they bucked urban living and embraced the need to *drive till you qualify* (for a home mortgage).

In the 1980s, Boomers could afford bigger, more expansive homes if they bought farther out where property costs were cheaper. Strip malls and shopping centers seemed to pop-up overnight, each circled by rings of parking lots. Some would say the sprawl was universal: as the square footage of homes increased, so did the expanses of big box stores and chain restaurants, and, coincidentally, the consumer appetites and waistlines of Boomers. Transportation and housing have become so entwined for Baby Boomers that it is difficult for them to imagine a different lifestyle.

The society is changing though, as the Age of Sprawl gives way to a "less-traveled" Internet based culture. Baby Boomers, who are more comfortable with their cars than most things digital, will come to recognize that they must find new ways to travel and maintain their mobility. Importantly, as they grow older, infirmities will make them less capable drivers. While Baby Boomers are not all going to "move downtown" they will need to seek alternatives. Today, 21 percent of the population over age 65 does not drive. Again, this is a gendered issue, since older women stop driving at an earlier age than men.

There are more changes in store for Boomers, as the Age of Sprawl gives way to the Internet based culture. The real-estate market, always attempting to anticipate where people want to work and live, is reactive to these trends. In a simple world, the Boomers would cash-out their properties and expect the next generation to be willing buyers that would step into their suburban footsteps, or more aptly, suburban driver-seats. However, the Boomers did not step into their parents more urban residences, and so they should not expect the next generation of Digital Natives to seek out their properties either. There is a sea-change taking place in terms of what is a desirable property and where younger people want to live. We detail these changes throughout the book.

Since the Boomers are a generation used to continual change, they will have to accept that they are going to retire in a very different time and place than they imagined. On the horizon are many technological changes, from robots to self-driving vehicles. Digital inventions are already beginning to impact the value of real estate, driving up prices in some locations, and down in others. Although it may seem improbable to Boomers, the smart phone and Internet are luring young people to reside in more urban areas, where they can claw back time for studying, socializing, and exercise, instead of drive-time spent commuting back and forth.

The younger generation is also doing a rethink about the costs of the drive time, both monetary and psychic. They are making a connection between physical health and commuting. They are also recognizing that walking and biking may provide a better lifestyle, even when they have families of their own. Equally important, we are on the cusp of a new transportation trend that will have vast, unknown consequences. Right now, the driverless car by Google (and others) seems like just another quirky idea from an über-high-tech firm. In fact, the U.S. government has been advancing the technology for many years by funding start-ups in universities and sponsoring competitions among engineering students. The technology of the driverless car has been realized; now it is a matter of settling the political and social agenda that will accompany it. It is still early, but automated vehicles present new ways to rethink the landscape of cities and suburbs.

This innovation is of great importance to the Baby Boom generation. If the technology arrives in time, the driverless car may give a second wind to older people who choose to age in the suburbs. It will also reduce accidents and help relieve traffic congestion. Most importantly, these "greener cars" could put the decision back on the table, for all age groups, of where we choose to live.

With technology at the forefront, this book pursues answers to a few simple questions. For those buying or selling real estate the book spells out the fragile balance between housing and transportation.

These questions that this book will address include:

1. In light of the housing crash in 2007, have people who are on the verge of retirement saved enough? Or are they depending on their homes as a nest egg to fund their retirement? What are the impacts for their personal welfare, and for the larger economy?

2. Can the current generation of older people age well in their suburban housing stock? Do they have sufficient mobility when they are able to

drive less? Can technological changes and fixes help Boomers age in far-flung suburbs?

3. Suppose older people choose to sell their suburban homes and move to more densely populated areas, or age-friendly communities? Who are the likely buyers for their homes? With newer technology, are suburban homes still desirable, or will there be a vast real estate sell-off?

4. How can younger people, the so-called Digital Natives, deal with an older population of Boomers (their parents) who wish to age in place but lack transportation? And, will Digital Natives be impacted if Boomers "bank on the house" (i.e. spend it) for retirement income, leaving a pittance for the next generation?

This book does not give financial advice nor will it resolve whether people should age at home, move to smaller homes, or join a retirement community. But it will provide background and insights to spur that discussion. Although it is directed at Baby Boomers, my hope is that it stimulates inter-generational discussion: if Mom and Dad, who are still healthy, do not relocate to a more walkable neighborhood soon, who is going to chauffeur them when they are no longer safe drivers? And, what if there are no kids? Nearly 20 percent of the Boomers are childless. The next generation may have even greater worries if their elders have "bet the house" on a reverse mortgage. These mortgages could quickly wipe out the house they are living in, or the inheritance they were counting on.

Aging in Suburbia is a wake-up call for a generation that has always been able to reinvent itself, and now faces, in its final chapter, its biggest challenge. The Boomers will experience major life changes, but they also have a window of opportunity to reinvent *how* and *where* they want to age.

CHAPTER ONE
GROWING UP WITH THE CAR

Brenda and Elliot are sitting on their patio at their home in Southeast Georgia, drinks in hand. They are enjoying the late sunset on this mid-summer night. Brenda is a petite brunette, now in her mid-sixties and her husband Elliott, is about five years older. They have been married since 1970 and have lived here in this house since their second and last child was born, way back in 1980. It is a spacious, suburban house with a two-car garage, a horseshoe shaped driveway, and a flat cement pad for parking the camper.

As she sips her drink, a cranberry-vodka cocktail, Brenda surveys the half-acre lawn, trimmed and weeded. The gardener has worked here for years and knows just what to do. Then she turns her attention to the pool. It's sparkling with aqua-blue water and ready for swimmers, but the children live too far away. They come back only once or twice a year, often at Christmas when it's too cold to swim. Then she turns her attention to Elliot's new RV camper, parked in the driveway. It was an expensive "toy" and now gas prices have shot up too. Moreover, Elliot's eyesight is getting worse, and she is not so sure that they should make their fall trip to the state parks in Utah. During last year's vacation, someone sideswiped the camper.

Brenda turns to Elliot to ask him about the trip - should they do it again this year? But, Elliot has pulled out his phone and doesn't hear. She guesses that he is browsing the lineup for the upcoming Georgia-Florida football game. Brenda leans back and thinks...this is the home that she and Elliot have loved so much. But he's getting older (not she!) and he seems to spend most of his time reading emails from the kids or watching sports. He is certainly not spending time puttering around the yard, driving the RV, or exercising in the pool.

Brenda puts down her drink, now half-empty. She resolves to look at the new townhomes in the project being built, just ten minutes away. Perhaps it would be an easy transition from here to there...

During their lifetimes, Baby Boomers, the generation born between 1946 and 1964, settled in newer suburbs that ring older cities, fueled the growth of the recreational vehicle (RV) industry, and made it fashionable to take family vacations in the car. The Boomer generation is often filmed "doing things" in their cars. We have all seen the images of cars parked end to end at Cape Canaveral to watch the Apollo lunar missions hurtling off into space. But perhaps the most famous image is that of the massive traffic jam in 1969 outside Max Yasgur's dairy farm, better known as Woodstock. When the next generation looks back, they will remark that whatever the Baby Boomers did, they did in cars, and wherever they went, traffic jams followed.

The Beatles captured this generational heartbeat in their 1975 song, "Baby You Can Drive My Car." The Beep/Beep song was prophetic for a generation that associated *driving the car* with *being a star*. As they get older, the Boomers will need to rely on others to drive them, or find different ways to get around. In an ironic twist, Paul McCartney, who is a few years older than the first Boomers, performed at the final, ultimate concert at Candlestick Park in San Francisco. Unfortunately, many of the fans that arrived by car were unable to park and spent the August evening circling the old park, stuck in traffic.

Many people on the verge of retirement say they plan to trade in their cars and get a vehicle that is more age-friendly. But, when asked about where they plan to live, the majority of respondents do not expect to make changes. In fact, when polled, three out of four Americans (75%) say they would like to age in place, and two in three (66%) want to stay in their local community. They expect that a few modifications will make their homes age-friendly for retirement. Most people do not see the connection between their homes and their transportation needs, particularly if they are still safe drivers.

So, instead, a large industry has developed around simpler changes to existing homes. These include safety modifications like heated driveways, non-slip floors and better lighting. A recent ad targeted to seniors asks, *Are you in love with your home...but afraid of your stairs?* Safety in the home is important, but it is not the fundamental change. The fundamental needs are more challenging to arrange, like the security of having people to rely on, safe and reliable transportation, and a sufficient retirement income.

Much of the challenge comes from the fact that the Baby Boom generation sanctioned a deep and long-lasting relationship between housing and transportation. Over the past fifty years, *where* we live and *how* we travel have become entwined like a braided rope. Only 17 percent of Boomers live in dense urban cities with mass transportation. Since 1960, the number of homes close to public transportation has declined. The hallmarks of the Baby Boom generation are two-car families, daily commutes of fifty minutes or longer, and weekends spent traveling in the car to shop, visit, or do errands. Boomers who are active today have difficulty projecting ten or fifteen years ahead and imagining a time when their vision begins to fail and their reaction times slow. Near-retirees plan out their financial and health care issues, but avoid thinking about the needs when they can no longer drive safely.

This is problematic, because as people age, they will not stay "wellderly," that is, "well" plus "elderly." The ability to be a safe driver declines, because a reduction in driver reaction time, vision, and hearing are all normal components of getting older. Before our country went on a suburban building spree, the aging population was less dependent on car travel. The elderly were fewer in number, and they were more likely to have retired in places they both lived and worked in—places where they could walk to shops and services. In the bigger cities, older people could access slower moving, above ground streetcars and buses.

Now, as a result of an earlier building spree, the Boomers have boxed themselves into suburbia. Suburbia may have been a desirable aspiration for them thirty years ago, but it is not well suited for an older car dependent population. Researchers at the National Institute on Aging published a paper in 2002 that estimated people will outlive their ability to drive by approximately seven to ten years. This estimate was made a few years ago, and did not consider the impact of a population that is growing more dependent on prescription drugs. These drugs often have side effects that reduce concentration and awareness, vital for safe driving.

This is a nightmare waiting to happen.

Problems of Aging in Place

The connection between housing and transportation is beginning to unravel. Both Baby Boomers and their adult children are impacted, and need to take account of what it means to age-in-place, when "the place" is suburbia. There are many considerations:

1. An estimated 70 percent of Baby Boomers live in areas served by limited or no public transit. If Boomers stay in their homes as they age and continue to drive their cars, do they put other drivers and pedestrians at risk? We have all heard of the elderly man or woman who can barely see over the dashboard and veers into adjacent lanes. When a senior is involved in a serious car accident with injuries, it receives

undue media attention. Boomers are good drivers, but there will be more accidents, and negative media stories, because of their sheer numbers. This may stigmatize their mobility but also help them individually to assess the risks.

2. Some Boomers assume that if they stay at home and cannot drive as much, services will come to their doorstep. For example, they hope that home health care will provide skilled nurses or doctors on call. The home health care is growing, but not in ways that Boomers might expect. Home health care expects to reach Boomers through "age independence technology," a byword for devices like wearable clothing with biosensors, pills that transmit biometric data, and nanny robots. This industry forecasts growth from 2 billion dollars today to 30 billion by 2020. So-called "nanny robots" will have multiple roles: one group will send daily health reports to a monitoring agency. A different set of bots will manage tasks in the

home that become too difficult like food preparation or cleaning. A third type may provide companionship and social interaction. Boomers need to assess whether they wish to age in place if they must engage with this new technology.

3. Another factor that makes it difficult to age in place is the physical effort needed to take care of homes. Seniors tend to overlook the expertise needed to maintain older homes, track the bills, evaluate vendors, and spot and fix repairs. Many suburban homes, built between 1970 and 2000, will get run-down and require multiple repairs. This responsibility will largely fall on the shoulders of older widows who outlive their spouses but stay in their homes. The expense of maintaining these homes, including rising insurance premiums, utilities and tax bills, will also fall on their shoulders.

4. Staying at home and mostly indoors overlooks an important health aspect: people who are more sociable and share their experiences will age better and live longer. Interaction with others is a component of good health. Regular exercise is too. In fact, recently published medical studies suggest that it is exercise, not puzzles, that maintain the aging brain. Many newer American suburbs discourage exercise because they were designed for cars not people. They lack sidewalks and bike paths. The design flaw is the resultant need to pack up the bicycle or walking shoes in order to drive to exercise.

5. Baby Boomers have not worked out what will happen when they are compromised as drivers and need to ask for help. Amazon and home grocery delivery are not going to cover all of their needs, all of the time. The most likely pinch-hitters are their adult children. But, if the Boomers are childless, and nearly 20 percent are, or, if their children live in other places,

driving Mom and Dad is not feasible. Neighbors, acquaintances, and civic groups may be available but asking others for rides may seem like an imposition.

6. Most of all, a generation of Boomers has expected to use their real estate as a "nest egg." Financial advisors estimate that at least 20 to 30 percent of Boomers have not saved enough, and, as of 2007, home equity represented 80 percent of the total wealth for a quarter of the homeowners over age 62. Prior to 2007, Boomers contributed to the run-up in real estate prices as they bought larger homes with bigger loans. The expectation was that these homes would continue to increase in value and help fund their retirement. Unfortunately, many Boomers will find that they have overcommitted and don't have a comfortable nest egg to retire on. The AARP reports than more than thirty-four percent of Americans age fifty plus use credit cards to pay basic living expenses,

including their mortgage because they do not have enough savings. One of the most startling trends is the number of people carrying mortgage debt as they age. In 1989, 37 percent of those aged fifty-five to sixty-four were carrying mortgage debt. In 2010, the rate rose to 54 percent for this age group and was 41 percent among those, ages 65 to 74.

Who Wants Old Homes?

Boomers anticipate that "when the time comes," they will sell their homes to the next generation and move to a more suitable property. They expect a pent-up demand from buyers, similar to when they bought. After all, for more than seventy years, the American Dream has been synonymous with home ownership. President Herbert Hoover promoted it as a social good for families; Lyndon Johnson imagined it would combat urban decay; and Bill Clinton made homeownership rates a centerpiece of policy.

While the American Dream still lives on, the

suburban homestead no longer matches this desire as well as other property types. New buyers would prefer different types of homes. It will not be easy for Boomers to move on even if the housing market is improving. There are many reasons for this:

1. Suburban homes do not complement new lifestyles. Only 54 percent of the adult population is married and single-person households rose to 27 percent in 2010. These households do not require big, stately four-bedroom homes with center staircases. There is also an increasing trend for people, both single and married, to be permanent renters.

2. Suburban homes are viewed as "energy hogs." This pejorative metaphor refers to both the 1980's style suburban home and the excess car travel required to reach it. The generation that was raised in suburbia is questioning if it is desirable to live so far from their jobs or

schooling, and be totally dependent on personal cars. They associate this older lifestyle with air pollution, climate change, and energy dependence.

3. This same generation is rethinking how cars and transportation fit into a modern lifestyle. A younger, urban generation is reducing their car ownership and favoring taxi services like Uber and Lyft that can be summoned on smart phones. They know it is unsafe to phone or text while driving. But, as a passenger in an Uber vehicle, or on buses and streetcars, they can use the travel time to stay online. With this newly found mobility, they view the single-driver car as a dinosaur that predates urban villages with their walkable streets and healthy cycling.

4. For trendsetters, suburbia is beginning to look dull and washed out, while cities are more edgy. This trend grows out of the Internet economy and a cultural shift to things digital (Chapter

Seven). Young professionals seem to lead the pack as they choose to live in the city but commute (often by bus) to their jobs in Silicon Valley. Meanwhile, major tech firms, once established in suburbia, are relocating their headquarters back to the cities.

5. Maintaining a suburban home can be time intensive. The younger generation is more intent on networking, training, and travel, possibly because jobs are scarce and they need to keep current to remain competitive in today's job market. They are less willing to allocate their limited free time to home maintenance and repairs. Unlike the Boomers, they do not foresee a payoff from their sweat equity.

The Financial Wake-Up Call

If Boomers can't sell their homes for the top-dollar that they expect, many will need to seek out financial help to stay at home. Reverse mortgages, which we discuss in Chapter Five, were once viewed as the savior for elders who ran short on cash but wanted to stay put. Financial lenders are now reevaluating the reverse mortgage because so many of these mortgages defaulted during the housing bust. As a result, lenders when underwriting these loans today are more likely to acknowledge that the value of homes could fall, not rise.

When did these changes take place? And, how could they happen to such a fun-seeking generation that bopped to "Baby You Can Drive My Car?" One answer is that Boomers were born into the boom era of transportation technology. Their lifestyles and their homes were centered toward four wheels. That period, like the unwinding of the Detroit economy, is coming to a close. An economy centered on transportation and things mechanical is being pushed aside by the arrival of the Digital Age. It portends changes in where people work and how they value their leisure time and their homes.

Demography, the science of population numbers, is also the determiner of property values. The age distribution of a population, plus factors like the birth rate, family size, and immigration establish how many potential buyers there are for homes and if it is a buyers' market or a sellers' market. The good news for the Baby Boomers is that the U.S. population is growing. Although there are 78 million Boomers, there are even more young people. Younger buyers, ages twenty-five to forty-six, have a combined population of 164 million, and that is a rich vein for future household formations. It is also noteworthy that this population uptick is coming from immigration.

The not-so-promising news is that these potential buyers, demographic cohorts known as Generation Y and the Digital Natives, are marrying later, if they marry at all, having fewer children, and opting to live in more urban areas. Any one of these factors (later, smaller, urban) would rattle a real estate market that is weighted toward large-lot suburban homes. Taken together, the rattle is measurable on the Richter scale. These patterns will ripple through home values and make it difficult for near-retirees, particularly those in more remote suburban homes to count on their real estate as a retirement asset.

There are currently about 75 million Boomers in the United States and it is said that 6,000 people a day reach age sixty-five. The Boomers own roughly 37 million homes. Three-quarters of these homes are in the suburbs or beyond, fringe developments at the edge of a metropolitan area. Homes locked into automobile use will be less favored as we move from a car-centric economy to a digital one.

Consider the follow scenarios, excerpted from news stories. The stories are presented in chronological order, the first from a Florida development firm, dated 2003, before the recession. The second news item, after the economy tanked, is from a 2011 Internet posting, commenting on seniors' relocations. The third and fourth items are a snapshot of current financial options.

Dateline: Florida, Del Webb (2003):

Boomers don't want to move to a less expensive part of the country when they retire but will actually do so when the time comes. This will be their salvation for not having saved enough. When the mutual fund industry says you can't retire on less than 70 percent of your preretirement income, the boomers will say "Not me. I'm going to figure it out."

Dateline ("viable opposition" blogger (2010):

Unlike the short-term temporary meltdown in house prices created by the subprime mortgage issue of the past two years, this long-term demographic price correction could have a permanent impact on the housing market.

Dateline: Wall Street (2013):

Many baby boomers ...will need to consider how their homes and the value locked inside will help finance their retirement years. Reverse mortgages, which essentially allow people to use their homes as an A.T.M. could become an integral part of many retirees' financial plans, especially those who are short on cash but do not want to move. Right now, practically anyone who is breathing can qualify for a reverse mortgage- no underwriting or credit scores necessary. But that might be about to change.

Dateline: Ferguson, MO (2013):

(RHO Properties (a.k.a. "HomeVestors")...is known for its advertising slogan "We Buy Ugly Homes." It is said that half of the homes are from relatives who need to settle the family homestead. *"Losing a parent is always difficult ... My mother stayed in her home probably longer than she should have...it took me several months to look over her home and make some decisions about repairs she had not done in the last five years...that's when I saw the HomeVestors billboard..."*

Demographics at the Source

Demographics are not easy to grasp, so the press has distilled generational concepts into bite-sized terms like Baby Boomers, Generation X, and Generation Y, also known as Digital Natives, Millennials, and Echo Boomers. Each of those labels describes groups of people born within a defined range of dates. Very broadly, each group is thought to share commonalities that distinguish them from the groups born during a different time period. Generation X or Echo Boomers are the cohort born between roughly 1965 and 1980, and Generation Y or Millennials arrived between 1980 and 2000. The youngest of the Millennials, born after 1990, are sometimes called Digital Natives, a group we discuss in Chapter Seven. Baby Boomers, the 78 million born before the computer age, are depicted, in graphic terms, to be a population bulge moving through the digestive system of a rattlesnake. In 1964, the youthful Baby Boomers accounted for 37 percent of the U.S. population. Although the Boomers had barely shed their cloth diapers, the housing industry and builders could predict "boom times" ahead.

Chart I: The Population in 1960 (U.S. Census)

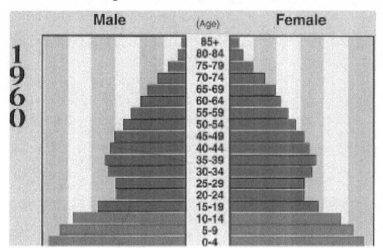

As the cohort of Boomers moved through their life cycle, they strained local hospitals, public schools, colleges, and finally, the labor force. In the 1980s, a much cited economics research paper by Mankiw and Weil predicted a tsunami-like impact of Boomers on the housing market. By 1990, the youngest of the

Boomers was age twenty-six, and the oldest had reached middle age, forty-four, well into their house-buying years.

Chart II: The Population in 1990 (U.S. Census)

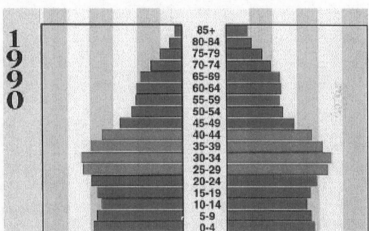

Notice that as the Boomers age and dominate the top of the population profile, the shape of the population graphic uncannily morphs from a triangle shape, wide at the base, to one that resembles a tall multi-story home (Chart III). In 2020, there will be 71 million Boomers, and they will represent about 23 percent of the U.S. population. By 2030, they are projected to represent one in five, about 59.8 million people. The Boomer cohort will "cease" after 2060, when only 2.4 million are projected to survive. Between now and then, there will be many, many homes for sale.

Chart III: The Projected Population in 2020 (U.S. Census)

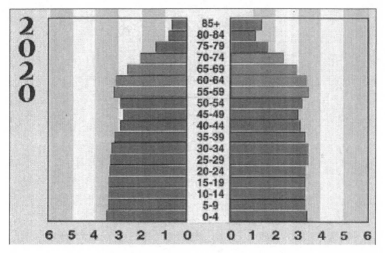

The Boomers and older age groups today are only a third of the U.S. population, but they own 60 percent of the owner occupied properties. They are a formidable economic force because of their real-estate holdings. As older age groups unwind their properties, they will impact the entire economy. One conservative estimate predicts that 26 million homes owned by Baby Boomers will come up for sale by the year 2030. Other estimates inflate this number up to 40 million homes.

Table 1: Who Owns Homes? Owner-Occupied Homes by Age Group

Age Category	U.S. Population in 2012 (1)	Percentage who own homes (2)
Age 0-20	26.3%	0.1%
Ages 21-34	20.6%	10.7%
Ages 35 to 49	19.8%	29.1%
Ages 50 to 65	19.5%	35.7%
Ages 66 to 75	7.6%	13.6%
Ages 76+	6.1%	10.8%

Source: (1) Sandra Colby and Jennifer Ortman, "The Baby Boom Cohort in the United States: 2012 to 2060." Current Population Reports. U.S. Census Bureau. Note: the age category used by the Census is 0 to 19, but the data for home ownership is 0 to 20.
(2) 2008-2012 American Community Survey Public Use Micro Data Sample (Owner Occupied Household Units) (n=75,239,229)

Another issue made evident by the census charts is the gender divide. Today's life expectancy is eighty-one years for women and seventy-six years for men. Women outlive men by about five years. Will so many elderly women be able to maintain these homes? Will they wish to live alone in big, empty homes?

Gray Homes Meet Modern Demographics

One of the hardest issues for Boomers to grasp will be that their homes are, well, "homely." In the chapter on suburbia and children (Chapter Six) we observe that the suburbs were designed to serve traditional families, like Hollywood's Ozzie and Harriet Nelson with a stay-at-home mother and two young sons. But, the real inhabitants, the Boomers, had 1.8 children instead of 2.0. There was no stay-at-home mom because Harriet worked full time, and the real Nelsons seldom met other neighbors or socialized. The real Nelsons were at home together only in the evenings or on weekends because they commuted to jobs that were far away. At home, they were more likely to play in their backyard than in front. There were few opportunities to meet the neighbors in a neighborhood lacking sidewalks.

While the Nelson family "lived" on a set in Hollywood, the Boomers spread across the country. They have migrated from urban areas in the Northeast and Midwest and settled in parts of the country that were previously more rural and less populated. The South seems to have attracted the newest homes and greatest sprawl (Table 2). Boomers followed jobs in the 1980s and 1990s and settled in these warmer climes. During the recession, the Boomers stayed in place, and it is plausible that they will be less likely to move to traditional, warmer retirement spots like South Florida or Arizona.

Table 2: Baby Boomer Population by Region, 2006 (U.S. Census)

Rank	Region	Number of Baby Boomers
1	South	28,060,126
2	Midwest	17,569,066
3	West	17,421,670
4	Northeast	14,929,434

Since the Boomers began buying homes, new construction has turned out bigger homes, but the families that live in them have been getting smaller. Demographers label this a "spatial mismatch." Table 3 puts some numbers on the spatial mismatch and we see how family sizes have shrunk, while home sizes have bloated. One blogger, noting how homes have super-sized, says that the average Canadian home from the 1950s is around the same size as today's three-car garage!

When Baby Boomers start to sell their homes, realtors will need to match these large, suburban properties to willing buyers. Couples with one child and single householders, whether divorced or unmarried, simply do not need the additional space. They are unlikely to be talked into bigger homes since these homes limit their ability to spend freely, travel, and be flexible when a better job comes along. Recognizing this, realtors are pinning their homes on a different market. They hope that new immigrants might take up the slack.

A bright spot might be the Hispanic market, which comprises about 15 percent of the population and have more children. The counter argument is that they cannot afford these large family-friendly homes *unless* the prices drop. There is also hope that other immigrant groups with more kids and multi-generational households will be buyers.

Studies predict that if a net immigration of 1.2 million people per year continues, then by 2020 they will form about 3.4 million new households. That is good news for Baby Boomers who will need to find buyers. But, first-time buyers may not see suburban homes as their American Dream. Typically, they prefer urban properties that provide a rental income. The news gets worse for Boomers who own large suburban homes with many bedrooms: in the most recent U.S. census, the only increase in household size occurred among family heads that had a high school degree or less.

Table 3: Big Homes and Small Families

	1969-1973	1989-1993	2009-2012
Average household size	3.14	2.63	2.55
One-person households (living alone)	17%	25%	27%
Households with 4 + people	37%	26%	23%
Stay-at-home mothers (married w/ child < 15)	44%	25%	26%
Married couple households with their own children	40%	26%	20%
Married couple households with no children	30%	30%	29%
New home (median sq. ft.)	1,525	1,905	2,169
New home (average sq. ft.)	1,660	2,080	2,443

Note: The data in this table is compiled from the US Census for 1970, 1990, and 2010. However, the percentages for stay- at- home mothers and the average/median house size are collected during a different time period, generally one or two years earlier/later. The data sources and the reporting year are listed in the references for this chapter.

Are Gray Homes "The Right Stuff?"

Demographics, financial markets and transportation are not in alignment for Baby Boomers. In recent years there has been a triple whammy of job loss, underfunded pensions, and spiraling health care costs. Recent polls of seniors age sixty-plus show that half are concerned that their savings are not sufficient, and one-third are worried about being able to stay in their current homes. The Boomers' average home price dropped by approximately 13 percent, from a high of $305,000 in 2006 to around $265,000 in 2012. We will revisit the numbers in Chapter Five, but since the financial crisis, real estate values have risen only moderately in many markets, crushing hopes of "banking on the house."

Baby Boomers are sellers. They are part of a large generational cohort, selling suburban homes over a twenty-year span. The buyers for these homes sit at the other end of the demographic cycle. There are many of them, which is good news. But their numbers are not a function of a high birth rate or a prosperous economy. The population growth has come from a liberal immigration policy.

In the next chapter, we look at the implications of sprawling large-lot houses. They seem reminiscent of those Detroit-styled cars from the 1960s with capacious trunks and stylish fins. The essential problem is that what is stylish and desirable in one period may seem excessive or downright silly at a future time. Housing stock is durable, while the population and its tastes change. This notion may be a shockwave for Boomers. Their beloved suburban homes may not be the "right stuff" to younger buyers.

Unlike cars, which we can dynamically replace as our family needs expand, for example, from sports car to mini-van, living arrangements are more fixed. If we decide to age in place, then we are likely to age in homes that cannot be optimized for older people and may incarcerate us in new ways.

There is an even more fundamental problem that accompanies aging in place. We expect our daily routines to remain relatively the same and there will be stability as we shop, do errands, and go places. As we move into the Digital Age, the shopping malls are closing, local businesses are being shuttered, and there is tremendous upheaval on commercial fronts (see Chapter Seven). In many areas, our safe and familiar family homes are, to borrow a recent movie title, "No Country for Old Men." "No Country for Old Men" knows no gender boundaries and is even more divisive for older women.

CHAPTER TWO
DRIVE TILL YOU QUALIFY

The saga of Brenda and Elliot continues. In this chapter we roll back to when they bought their first house. It is not the one they live in today. We look at how the economy changed for the better and they were able to afford this newer home and many more things... like the swimming pool installation and Elliot's RV. Things changed yet again—the economy soured. We compare houses "then" and houses "now".

The Boomers Build a Nest Egg

Following World War II, most Boomers were born into moderate circumstances; they were not babes with silver spoons in their mouths. But as a generation, they touched their share of the precious metal. The generation born between 1946 and 1964 experienced a long run of financial expansion, as the economy grew for more than twenty-five years. Compared with the Millennials, Boomers racked up considerably less debt for higher education, and they had more secure jobs— until the current recession. Baby Boomers weren't just largest generation in history; they were also the wealthiest.

However, they have not held on to that wealth as successfully as their parents did. There are, of course, vast disparities in income but in 2011, the median net worth of Baby Boomers was 8 percent lower, at $143,964, than those seventy-five and older. Some of this wealth may return if the stock market ticks upward but the Social Security Administration projects that only 40 percent of the Baby Boomers will be able to maintain three-quarters or more of their pre-retirement income when they retire. Part of the loss has occurred because of pensions: only 10 percent of the

Boomers will collect an outside pension, compared with 37 percent of today's elderly.

The financial predicament of the Boomers also reflects their generosity and their willingness to support charities, churches, and extended families. However, the spending did not stop there. Many have also used their homes as a piggy bank to finance other life-style needs and they have taken on substantial debt from home equity loans, second mortgages, credit cards, and personal loans. As long as the housing market ticked upward, and home equity grew, their debt obligations could be rolled forward.

A large proportion of household wealth is created from real estate, but the Baby Boomers have had an up-and-down relationship with both. In the 1970s, the oldest Boomers came of house-buying age, and they faced a shortage of housing stock. In the 1980s, as younger Boomers entered the housing market, double-digit interest rates prevailed. As the following chart makes evident, Baby Boomers have enjoyed a downward ride with interest rates since then.

Chart IV: A Downward Ride With Interest Rates

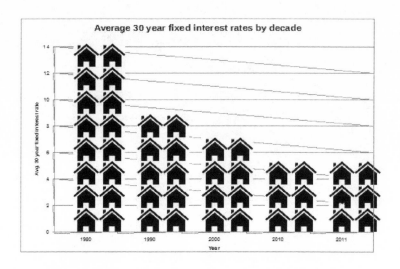

Buying Homes and Buying a Lot More

Mortgage rates and federal policy are entwined. After World War II, government policy played an important role in launching new suburbs. Back then, the GI bill regulated government-insured mortgages in a way that they could be used only to buy newly constructed homes—this encouraged growth in undeveloped areas outside the cities.

Most Boomers, however, did not qualify for VA loans. But, with the high interest rates in the 1980s, there was a pent-up demand for homes, as Boomers were marrying and starting families. This time federal policy did not spur the growth of the suburbs. Instead, it was that soul mate of Detroit, the car.

An ethos emerged that you could *drive till you qualify*: Boomers could purchase "more house" if they bought at a distance from cities and their jobs, offsetting double-digit mortgage rates. The need was substantial: an average house that sold in 1985 for $90,000 with a 19 percent down payment had a monthly payment of $875—that's $1,642 in 2014 dollars! But, there were high costs associated with the *drive till you qualify* that were seldom recognized at the time. An implicit cost was their time: the Boomers traded the time spent commuting by car for some other activity, say getting exercise, meeting their neighbors, or attending school and community functions. The other cost was more explicit: commuting long distances was expensive, so the Boomers traded down to smaller, more fuel-efficient vehicles.

In reaction to the high interest rates and a shortage of suitable properties, a number of Boomers did not actually become homeowners until the 1990s. By this point they had one or two children and sought larger, suburban properties. These far-flung suburban homes were still relatively quick to reach because they coincided with the completion of the National System of Interstate and Defense Highways, better known as the highway-building program championed by President Dwight Eisenhower. The construction began in 1956, and the original portion was finally completed in 1991. The new roads made it easier to reach the far-flung suburbs and they had yet to be filled with traffic congestion. It wasn't evident at the time that this colossal road-building project had shifted all transportation budgets—federal, state, and local dollars, away from mass transportation and into highways and roads. The consequence of this was to lock the suburbs into the car dependency we know today.

After buying their first homes at relatively high interest rates, the Boomers saw the economy change and started refinancing. By 2000, interest rates moderated, and new loans had looser down-payment requirements. This helped Boomers keep more cash in their pockets. It also helped stimulate larger home purchases, vacation properties, and the refinancing of existing ones. New car purchases and car leasing surged. The Baby Boomers eagerly acquired the vehicles needed to participate in the growing sprawl of shops, commuter centers, and entertainment venues.

Around the same time, federal policy was revamped to extend home ownership to new income groups and minorities. Like the earlier GI bill, federal policy and mortgage rates were again entwined. Rates dropped and lenders qualified people with a less predictable income stream who might have otherwise remained renters. As house prices bubbled up it seemed like everyone could acquire some real estate. That outlook had briefly abated in the 1990s when house prices dipped regionally. But a realignment of the savings and loan industry and a surge of refinancing seemed to jump-start the flagging market.

House sales continued to grow after 2000 although the vast majority of Baby Boomers had already bought a starter property and settled into home ownership.

Since the initial demand from their demographic growth had been met, the new housing surge seemed to come from Boomer's trading up to second homes or an investment property. The demand also came from the federal policy to expand home ownership to new buyers. In hindsight, lower interest rates could have encouraged Boomers to reduce their mortgage payments in view of their future retirement. While some did, the majority seemed to have spent the monthly savings from refinancing and then added new debt with home equity loans.

Between 2000 and 2006 the lower interest rates and escalated property values spiraled to create a "wealth effect." The scope of wealth effects is a topic of longstanding interest among economists. Stripped to its basic terms, it suggests that Boomers felt financially better off and consumed more as they saw the value of their homes rise. One of the aspects of a wealth effect is that people need to sell their homes to maximize the real gains—but they can consume *indirectly* by borrowing. Economically, from 2000 through 2006, homes appreciated by as much as 72 percent according to the Case-Shiller index, and "just" 34 percent according to a government one. As the economy prospered, Boomers were confident about purchasing home accessories, furniture, recreational vehicles, and nice cars. They also spent amply on schools and tourism. The numbers say it all: credit card balances for the cohort aged fifty-five to sixty-four grew from $2,900 in 1989 to $6,900 in 2007. Households were piling on two sources of borrowing: mortgage debt and personal debt.

A nationwide spending spree developed. Kitchen and bathroom remodeling, home decorating, and home goods all flourished. Big box stores like Home Depot, Best Buy, and Bed Bath and Beyond came of age with the Baby Boomers. These stores were located within reasonable driving distance of residences and catered to drivers with their acres of free parking. Before they could shop online, these stores served as "idea factories," inspiring Boomers with things from A (appliances) to Z (zinnia plants sold seasonally in the likes of Home Depot garden centers). Some of the excesses of home decoration may be fancifully remembered as hot tubs, outdoor storage sheds larger than one-bedroom apartments, and Halloween decorations that morphed front yards into spooky cemeteries! In line with purchasing demand, the average Home Depot store grew from only 60,000 square feet at its first two stores in 1979 to an average of 105,000 square feet.

Locked into Suburbia

The Baby Boom generation changed where we lived, how we shopped, and what we needed to shop for. Their large, expansive house sizes locked the Baby Boom generation into a need to shop for more things, more often. As the number of single-family residences increased, there was a steep decline in building rates for new apartments and multifamily homes. After being under-built for many years, there is currently a resurgence of construction for condos, apartments, and multifamily homes. With new multifamily units being added, and older suburban homes ready to sell, there may be a buyer's market.

While interiors are important, it is the location of the homes that tells the full story. Since the *drive till you qualify* nicely coincided with the completion of the new interstate highway system, there was little thought to public transportation. The earliest American suburbs, like Framingham, Massachusetts, were designed around streetcar and rail systems, before the car. Somewhat later suburbs, like Levittown, New York, were established when families had only one car and it was still considered useful to be near a rail line. But, the newest suburbs, like the ones favored by the Baby Boomers, were completely car-dependent to the extreme that many neighborhoods even lacked sidewalks. With their affinity for cars and dual-income households the suburbs sprawled.

As the Boomers sprawled, so did neologisms (newly coined phrases or words) to describe the growth. Exurbs, from the 1950s, described a ring of prosperous communities beyond the suburbs that were commuter towns. Edge city was a term popularized in 1991 to describe a concentration of business, shopping, and entertainment outside a traditional downtown in what had previously been a residential or rural area. Boomburb, another neologism, described an area of explosive growth in an edge city having more than 100,000 residents and maintaining double-digit growth between 1970 and 2000. The homes surrounding the exurbs, the edge cities, and boomburbs are not of a single form, but often share in common these characteristics:

1. Low density development
2. Detached family homes with lawns and attached garages
3. Residents are car dependent—they need automobiles. Walking and bicycles are not practical for errands and shopping trips.
4. Stores and activities that are in close proximity still require driving because the areas are separated by barriers like busy roads or fences.

5. Strip malls, big box stores, and malls are the primary shopping centers. Some employment may be located in these shopping centers, but most workers have a twenty-five- to fifty-minute commute, typically to office parks or in some cases, cities.

Let's briefly examine the last item. The oldest suburbs, which developed at the turn of the nineteenth century, were built so that commuters could walk from home to a streetcar or train, usually within a one-quarter or one-half mile distance. The 1950s suburbs, like Levittown, were still proximate to a train line, and added a parking lot for commuters who drove to the station. The two-car, Boomer family changed things again. It allowed offices and jobs to spread out in all directions. Between 1970 and 2000 vast tracts of open land and farms were turned into bedrooms, and metropolitan areas covered almost twice as much land as they did at the start. The high-density walking city of 1900 was replaced by the medium density-driving city of 2000. The lower density and longer distances made it impractical to serve suburban areas with a decent level of public transportation, even for trips to work.

Locked into Lifestyle

In the following chapters we will assess the outlook for these suburban neighborhoods since three-quarters of the Boomers say they wish to age in place. Will these neighborhoods still be coveted places to live, and are they suitable for Boomers who are no longer commuting to jobs? Suburban homes, with an average size of 2,200 square feet, are getting emptier, as grown children (eventually) move out. In future chapters we note that many things are changing, even the concept of a home office, once a refuge for weary commuters. Now the home office can be anyplace with Wi-Fi and a connection to cloud storage so there is less need to set up a physical space.

To introduce that fundamental change, we will pretend to be a realtor who is going to sell you a home in two different time periods. In Table 4, the leftmost column has the realtor's talking points if they were selling to a Baby Boomer in 1985 or 1995. It describes all the things we have come to love about a suburban home. The rightmost column has the realtor's talking points for an older client. The real estate agent is convincing the Baby Boomers that their suburban home is no longer suitable, and they should move to a closer-in, more age-friendly community. The realtor may be particularly dogmatic that the Baby Boomer should move for purely economic reasons as well. Boomers have lived in their present homes for an average of 14 years, and have had time to build up home equity, despite the housing crash of 2007. When an owner builds home equity, outstanding mortgages and liens can be paid off, leaving cash on the table for something new!

Table 4: Talking Points— Then and Today

Real estate agent talking points:	Talking Points to a 45-year-old Boomer	Talking Points to a 65-year-old Boomer
Suburban location	The home is my sanctuary. It is private and exclusive.	It is hard to drive. You can't go out at night.
Big mortgage	This is your financial social security.	This home will not work as a cash-cow ATM!!
Square footage	There's room enough to spread out.	There's too much space to take care of.
Utilities	Just power up! Often, all electric.	The utility bills are supersized.
Taxes	Taxes support schools, parks, and police.	Too many new taxes. Unpredictable costs.
Entertaining friends	Chef's kitchen and barbecue	Prefer to be closer to restaurants/take-out.

Real estate agent talking points:	Talking Points to a 45-year-old Boomer	Talking Points to a 65-year-old Boomer
The luxuries	You have a built-in TV, big family room, hot tub, home office, more...	Don't use media room or hot tub, or gadgets. A real luxury is time and $$ for travel and seeing grandkids.
Home repairs	Ideal for D.I.Y. weekend projects.	You'll need to call in handymen and fix things all the time.
Big yard	The kids will play outside on the nice lawn.	The yard is a pain to maintain... snow, weeds, mud and bugs.
Neighbors	They come and go.	Would like to know 'someone' nearby to call....in case.
No sidewalks No bike path	Not so vital.	It's hard to stay fit just staying at home.
Neighborhood	Great mall shopping to drive to.	You can't walk to anything.

In Chapter One, we introduced what demographers call a "spatial mismatch." Houses are too big for our shrinking family size. It is not evident that there will be many buyers for the big, expansive, suburban homes that Baby Boomers built. Suburban homes exalted the nuclear family, but that is no longer the American norm. Fifty-eight percent of married couples have no children, and another 16 percent have just one. That leaves just one-quarter, 26 percent, with two or more kids. Of course, there are many new family types, like unmarried parents who live together, and single moms and dads. But the less traditional the family structure, the more likely that they will not want a giant four-bedroom house with a central staircase, double garage, and a lawn that needs to stay manicured. More people are choosing to live alone during some or all of their adult years. The single exception is immigrant families—as we noted in the first chapter, these families are large and growing. However, new immigrants are concentrated in urban areas where they hold jobs, and they are less able to pay the full sticker price for big suburban homes.

The second spatial mismatch, which we explore in future chapters, is more complicated. It is also more interesting than sheer numbers. Our hypothetical Boomer at age sixty-five has had a long chat with a realtor (see Table 4). The features that were once so attractive in his or her suburban home now seem fusty and outdated. The options that seemed attractive to a forty-five year old are at best a hassle or at worst a liability in retirement: the big yard, once a great place for the kids to play, is now filling up with weeds. The custom kitchen with granite countertops is a waste of space when you're heating those microwave dinners.

If Boomers pop their heads outside the four walls of their homes, they'll notice strong headwinds of change. An Internet-centric culture is phasing out the car-centric one. Boomers are caught in the tailwind of this change. In the following chapters we will describe why they should expect to retire in very different times, even if within the same physical place.

CHAPTER THREE

TRANSPORTATION: "THE KEY" PROBLEM FOR BOOMERS

Ever since Brenda and Elliot bought their RV camper, it has been a showpiece they love to drive. Until now. Someone sideswiped the camper and the insurance company made Elliot enroll in safe-driver classes. Brenda is wondering whether their long driving trips are still feasible. It's probably just the RV, she reasons, "it's too big...they are safer in other type of vehicles".

Most Boomers will recall a coming-of-age movie from the 1970s called *American Graffiti*. Filmed in Petaluma, California, this car-centric flick makes it clear that the car was king. Some Baby Boomers might have even inferred that they were conceived in the backseat of a Chevy. Whatever the circumstances, there has always been an amorous relationship between Boomers and their automobiles.

While their parents (and occasionally grandparents) bought into the first suburban tracts designed for cars, the Boomers wholly reshaped the suburbs. They expanded one-car driveways to accommodate two or three cars, preferred paved streets to paved sidewalks, and even cherished a building style derisively nicknamed the "snout house." The snout, or garage, faced the street, while the people entrance was tucked off to the side.

In 1969, when the oldest Baby Boomers entered their twenties, nearly 70 percent of households had a single car, and only 30 percent of households with two adults owned two or more vehicles. Today, the numbers are reversed. Over the past four decades car ownership nearly tripled, travel rates more than doubled, and total mileage traveled grew twice as fast as the population. During this period, the two-worker family became the norm, and that explains much of the car-driving growth. Not surprisingly, it led to another norm: an expectation to drive everywhere. Even in

Boomers' near-retirement, this expectation thrives. The Boomer cohort logs nearly 17 percent more vehicle miles than other age groups. The cause is not clear: they may enjoy driving, so they take more trips, or they may have to drive, because they have settled in more remote, distant suburbs.

Boomers are used to spending time in their car. In 1980, the average commute time to work was just under 22 minutes. Commute time stretched as Boomers bought homes in the suburbs and exurbs, farther from their places of work. About 2 percent of the commuters made driving a daily marathon, a ninety-minute or longer commute.

There are several reasons that Boomers, as youths, could embrace the automobile with such flourish. For the half-century following their invention, cars were fidgety—you needed to know how to fix a flat tire, change the oil, jump dead batteries, and push a stalled vehicle off the road. That excluded many—notably women, the elderly, and busy people. Only in the 1960s and '70s did the service economy begin to make car maintenance more routine, and there grew a proliferation of car-care franchises like Jiffy Lube and Midas.

Meanwhile, as Baby Boomers came of house-buying age, two factors encouraged their likelihood to live farther out. One factor, which we highlighted in Chapter Two, was the *drive till you qualify* response to double-digit mortgage rates. Many Boomers found affordable construction to be farther away from urban centers. The additional costs of transportation, as well as the extra commute time, were not deal breakers. The second factor was the growth of the two-income family. For two-income households with frequent job changes, it made sense to locate near major highways and arterials. Such a decision had hidden costs that were not so evident at the time: personal costs like the time to travel, and social costs like accidents, energy dependence, land-use, and air pollution. More recently, there has been concern that long commutes contribute to stress, weight gain, and higher blood pressure.

Drive, Boomer, Drive!

Between 1970 and 2005 Boomers piled on vehicle miles the way Millennials and Digital Natives now seem to devour data bytes on the Internet—endlessly. For Boomers, the car opened a wide universe of travel for social visits, shopping, and filling leisure time. They were also the first generation of homeowners to acquire a second car. An unexpected outcome of these working families was even more driving, as they outsourced goods and services that were previously done at home. Many of these activities with the exception of childcare, are now being streamlined over smartphones.

A landscape enabled by the automobile had vast, unfathomed impacts: it is estimated that for each vehicle we own there are six parking spaces that are built for parking occasions at grocery stores, airports, shopping centers, churches, and so forth. While the number of parking spaces grew, jobs did not. Between 1990 and 2012, the total number of employees involved in the manufacture of motor vehicle and motor vehicle parts has decreased by 62 percent and 73 percent, respectively.

The gas crisis of the 1970s forged a fondness for Japanese cars, and their smaller, more efficient engines helped offset the travel costs for longer commutes. The air pollution seen in the 1950s and 1960s was in some ways tamed by the catalytic converter in 1975 and the mandate for cleaner burning fuels. Concurrently, automakers improved comfort, and car interiors achieved new standards as drivers spent more and more time in their vehicles. Today, the trend is toward smaller, hybrid vehicles, enabling long-distance commuters to stretch their budget. There is also an industry-wide recognition that car buying by Boomers has peaked and that is making car dealers search for younger markets.

Locked into Cars

The dominance of the automobile seeded its Achilles' heel as it edged out public transportation. When build-

72

ing permits were approved for the *drive till you qualify* housing subdivisions, almost no provisions were made for other travel modes. The public transit system was urban; it did not function well in low-density areas with a stretched array of shopping centers, fast food places, office parks and car lots.

Suburban tracts, built prior World War II, were not as car-centric. Houses were positioned within one-quarter- to one-half-mile walking distance of train or trolley stops, and local businesses clustered around the tracks. The sprawl of jobs and homes upended this model and displaced walking to stores and shops. The unintended consequences, like congestion and lack of neighborhood, were not foreseen. Initially, cars were depicted as a utopian machine that would liberate the masses from the daily bondage of place. The following quote ascribed to the invention of cars, from James Howard Kunstler, seems to parallel contemporary faith for an Internet enabled utopia.

"There was nothing like it before in history...It was assumed that cars would merely serve as wonderful useful accessories in the human habit... that they

would make the city a better place, and cure all the troubles of rural life, without altering the arrangement of things in either place."

For suburbs, the automobile offered a convenience that public transit has not achieved: door-to-door service. When you make multiple stops or what transportation planners call "chained trips," the car offers considerable time saving and ease over public transit. Planners like to speculate that if public transportation systems had continued to innovate over the past fifty years, they might have become a rival to the automobile. Instead, public transit seemed to be frozen in time. Vast amounts of public money financed a car-centric infrastructure of new highways, bridges, and roads instead. Transit operators were woefully underfunded; with their older technology they never solved how to efficiently run buses in and out of suburban neighborhoods, make multiple stops and pickups, and provide a quality of service to spread-out residential and commercial tracts.

Since public transit did not keep pace and still shows few innovations to leap forward, suburban areas limit the mobility of many groups, in addition to the elderly. These groups include the mentally and physically handicapped, teenagers old enough to get out but too young for a license, the suburban poor who cannot afford car expenses, and "fresh air" users who would like to walk or bike but are stymied by the lack of safe pathways.

What Drives the Future?

The "64 million-dollar question" is when Boomers are going to be added to this list. Can the suburban landscape, based on motoring, accommodate the mobility needs of aging Boomers? The needs are staggering: the AARP projects that by 2025 one in every five drivers will be over the age of 65. As people age, they often grow less mobile. In 2001, an estimated 23 percent of older adults were afflicted with mobility impairments. Specialists use the term "transportation disability" when a medical condition makes travel outside the home difficult. Many Baby Boomers are expected to face transportation disabilities because of chronic health conditions. Today, 21 percent of the population over age 65 does not drive.

For those who wish to age at home, transport is probably the biggest hurdle. While homes can be modified to accommodate the needs of aging, it is more difficult to modify our cars and our streets. Transportation will impact the quality of life as well as the simple ability to do everyday things. Even for the "wellderly," those aging in good health, transportation presents a conundrum. There are an increasing number of studies linking illness and obesity to the lower levels of physical activity. Newer suburbs lack alternative systems of navigation, like public transportation, sidewalks, and bike lanes. Sidewalks and bike paths have to be reinvented, because for nearly fifty years the car was king, and trumped the building and operation of all other transport.

This leads to several practical concerns for Boomers. Since public policy has been shortchanged, what are aging Boomers going to do? We will discuss the concerns as if we were in a town-hall meeting responding to an enraged citizenry.

Safety of Older Drivers

1. **Assume the Baby Boomers stay put in their existing homes and continue driving. Are they more likely, as older drivers, to be in accidents?**

Everyone seems to have stories of their aging relative or friend who has a car marred with dents or who came close to causing a road accident. When an older driver loses control and kills pedestrians and bystanders, the news story gets disproportionate coverage vis-a-vis accidents caused by teen drivers. In fact, teens are involved in more accidents when you examine per capita miles driven. However, poor teen driving is overshadowed by the fact that there will be so many older drivers in the future. By 2020 eight states will have 20 percent of their population age 65 and older: Florida, Maine, Montana, New Mexico, North Dakota, Vermont, West Virginia, and Wyoming.

Unlike teens, senior drivers tend to "self regulate" and cut back driving when they feel unsafe on the road—one bright spot of the demographics. Younger seniors drive less at night and reduce the length of their trips. As they get older, they voluntarily turn in the keys. These data, however, are based on observing older cohorts, who are now age 69 and older. Unlike Boomers, the older cohorts are likely to have familiarity with transit, as they grew up using other transport modes. The current generation of Baby Boomers may behave differently, since this is the first generation to define their lifestyles around the *drive till you qualify*.

A recent National Household Travel Survey found that Boomers were beginning to change their travel patterns, but in unexpected ways. Between 2001 and 2009, they took more trips in their car, yet these were shorter and closer to home. The interpretation is uncertain. It could reflect a desire to reduce driving, or it could have been a reaction to the bad economy curtailing air travel and more expensive vacations. In more recent national data, researchers find that the Baby Boomers are driving less, and women, who may be giving up their careers, have cut back in particular.

Gender and demographics present imminent problems for the Boomer generation. Older women outlive men, and they drive less. Today, despite vast changes in society, transportation statistics already show that women aged fifty to sixty-four drive less than men. In 2009, only 89 percent of women, aged fifty to sixty-four were drivers compared with 95 percent of men that age. For those ages sixty-five to seventy-five, this fell to 93 percent for men and 84 percent for women. Among women older than seventy-five, only 61 percent drove. This is a pernicious cycle for older women who then face more social isolation if they age in place and cannot drive.

Depending on Public Transit

2. Will public agencies provide more options assuming older drivers stay in their existing homes?

As people age, public transit becomes more difficult to use. Transit systems have been designed for an active population that can climb up and down steps, take just a few seconds to board and exit, stand when there are no open seats, and withstand jerky vehicle stops and starts. While these characteristics may be somewhat of an exaggeration, there is no doubt that riding public transit becomes more difficult with age and physical impairments.

Unless there is a vast re-think of how to provide public transportation, Boomers are at the mercy of existing senior programs, like Dial-A-Ride and paratransit. Paratransit typically uses a taxi or small bus that runs a more-or-less defined route to pick up and drop off passengers. In the United States, it is usually a government service under contract with local public transportation agencies.

Resources have gone to other transportation problems, and relying on these services is not going to be an option for many. Paratransit, for example, is required to serve only the seriously disabled, operate within a three-quarter-mile route that parallels existing transit, and then only during regular transit hours. Professor Sandy Rosenbloom, a national expert on senior transportation, says that putting faith in paratransit "is just perpetrating another scam on the elderly." There are currently many government agencies and senior groups that organize special shuttles, paratransit, and taxi vouchers for the elderly. But, almost all of these programs are instituted to reach a particular subgroup (e.g. the disabled, low income, or medical transport) rather than the larger transportation needs of a "wellderly" but aging population.

Home Based Services

3. Assuming older drivers stay in their existing homes, can services come to them?

The answer to this is a resounding "Yes"—the Internet has brought a surge of entirely new delivery and service-oriented businesses that go door to door. Amazon has pioneered shop-at-home services, and since 2007, the home delivery of goods has surged. Today, a competing Google delivery service is available in certain markets. The delivery of groceries, an established service that has been reinvented with the Internet, has had a fitful start, but is poised to grow near urban areas.

Very few medical doctors make visits to the home as they did at the turn of the century. However, Boomers who are technologically savvy can increasingly use video and receive treatments through a new branch of telemedicine. The delivery of medical services is improving: there are about 875,000 home health aides as of 2012 and employment is estimated to grow by 48 percent over ten years. This is timely since the largest growth of trip making among Boomers has been for medical care.

Almost everything material that a Boomer might need can be brought into his or her suburban home through home delivery or via a video channel. Electronic monitoring could scan for falls or other health issues and send for help. The advance of nanny robots (see Chapter One) works well with home delivery systems. Once home groceries have arrived at the doorstep, the nanny robot can bring them inside, restock the cupboard, even heat up simple meals and clean up.

However, Boomers will have to ask collectively, and individually, what personal price they will pay for these services. After leading such active lives, will they have an acceptable quality of life if they are confined to their homes with an occasional visit from a FedEx delivery person and the home health worker? Aging Boomers need to imagine what happens when they cut back on their driving, stay at home more, and cannot socialize in person. Will they be content? For a cohort that has equated mobility with recreation, this may be a difficult compromise.

Rethinking Mobility, I

4. Assuming older drivers stay in their homes, are there other alternatives?

The flexibility to rethink old problems in new ways is the hallmark of the Boomer generation, and it may also be the saving grace for their access and mobility. One simple idea links back to the Internet economy. The Internet has helped launch Airbnb, a runaway success that enables house letting for vacationers. "Carbnb" might be the next great Internet triumph. Here, Boomers would exchange rooms in their house for assistance with transportation. Those strapped to find suitable accommodations could match up with a Boomer who needs outside help. This arrangement, particularly suited to college towns, would pair younger people who have difficulty finding affordable housing with older people who have big homes and extra rooms but insufficient dexterity to drive.

Another spin on this are not-for-profit senior "villages" that band together, like Beacon Hill (www. Beaconhillvillage.org) to offer services including shared rides and rides on demand. The village model is arguably the most successful model for Boomers who wish to age in place. It is primarily staffed by volunteers, but has direct links to social services, and of course, transportation programs run by local agencies. There are other mobility networks too, both for-profit and non-profit, like ITN and Eldercare Locator.

Another option, but further out on the horizon, is to computer-assist cars so they self-propel like automated taxis. These so-called SAVs—shared autonomous vehicles—would take the driver out of the driving equation. A Boomer, living at home, would program the car (probably from a smartphone) with a location, and software would manage the rest of the trip. Shared autonomous vehicles may be the most functional option in the future to blend public and private transportation. SAVs would navigate large, spread-out suburban tracts, yet provide the familiar on-demand, personal, door-to-door service we know today.

Boomers will have to wait, though, because these vehicles are still in the testing stage. Insurance and liability issues are bound to slow their roll-out. Today, the vehicles that automakers currently have on the assembly line for seniors are more mundane; they have conventional options like larger-sized mirrors, backup cameras, higher-up seats to make it easier to get inside, and brighter night-time headlights.

Less obvious are the changes that could be done to the public road system to improve their safety. Transportation engineers who design the roadway infrastructure create intersections, exits, signage, and lane markings with the assumption that the average driver is between 30 and 40 years of age. Counties with many older people, say in parts of Arizona and Florida, design differently, and are most likely to improve their signage and lane markings. One of the biggest issues for older people, however, is the speed at which drivers travel. It is a long and unpopular battle to lower speed limits for safety reasons.

Rethinking Mobility, II

5. Assuming older drivers stay put in their homes, can they use the Internet and smartphones to improve their transportation options?

The Internet has changed how we do the most conventional things like buying an airline ticket or looking up a phone number. Even flagging a taxi is changing—riders can locate the nearest vehicle using a map on their smartphone.

Taxis have never served the suburbs well. Operating the vast tracts of suburbia makes the service expensive for drivers and vehicles. It is the same reason bus service seems to be threadbare in the suburbs. Part of the expense may be the business process: today, most communities award "taxi medallions" to the highest bidder, typically wealthy investors. They, in turn, rent taxis, those familiar yellow or green-striped vehicles, to drivers who must compete for routes. There are more people who want to drive vehicles than taxi medallions awarded, so this restricts the trade and bids up the cost for the end user. On the other hand, local governments claim that medallions protect passengers, and ensure they are riding in an inspected vehicle with a licensed driver. New taxi services in urban areas, like Lyft and Uber, have been competing with the government-run medallion model. In the new business model, vehicle owners drive their own personal vehicles provided they are screened and have sufficient insurance coverage. The driver can be full time but is more likely to be picking up passengers on an occasional basis. This new transportation business has blossomed with smart-phones since the key is to use the mapping service on the phone to match proximate vehicles with proximate passengers.

Entirely new services enabled by smartphones may provide a literal "way out" for Boomers. They may be able to organize more frequent and less expensive taxi services for the suburbs. The feasibility of operating car share services in suburban tracts is untested. If Boomers join a carshare service, they could downsize the number of cars they own, and surplus vehicles could be repurposed into the share car fleet. Since there would be many cars available to this network, the trick would be to locate drivers, not vehicles. It is estimated that one autonomous vehicle, that is, a self-driving car, could replace between eight and twelve private vehicles. This "tech" version of transportation, with cars summoned by smartphone, is more likely to appeal to Boomers than Dial-A-Ride and paratransit.

There is no reason that a senior network needs to follow the rules of Uber, of Dial-A-Ride, or of the existing taxi medallion system. Instead, Boomers could collectively buy shares in an entirely new car share service that served their age group and their suburban tracts. The upfront cost might be steep, but would be offset by savings from vehicle maintenance and insurance premiums.

Debunking the Drive Till You Qualify

We began this chapter by considering the romance of the automobile featured in the coming-of-age movie *American Graffiti*. That movie was prophetic. At the close the stars are having trouble moving on to college or other life chapters. One of the main characters ends the night as a chauffeur. In the movie sequel, yet to be made, that cast member could chauffeur on behalf of a senior network!

The absence of viable transportation options will place older Boomers in the unenviable position of deciding whether to cut back their activity levels, or to move to an area served by taxis, sidewalks, and public transit. What made Boomers' homes so desirable at one time—the privacy; the square footage; and large, leafy lots—also sowed disruptive seeds. These property features were gained at the expense of exhausting commutes and a built-in car dependence.

The generation that is ripe to buy suburban houses, those in the twenty-five-to-forty-five age group, is eliciting different tastes for home ownership and car travel. Teens today are delaying getting a driver's license, and only one-half (54 percent) get licensed by their eighteenth birthday. Rates for car ownership have decreased in urban areas as cash-strapped students and graduates choose smartphone contracts over monthly car payments. Meanwhile, the car is no longer king even among those with jobs. Young professionals are under pressure to work long weekday hours and occasional weekends. Their time budget makes it impractical to favor residences where they need to cut the grass, schedule home repairs, and drive to the store for a few groceries. Time budgets are only part of the equation.

The other part of the equation is cost: transportation is a key factor in the Millennials' decision to buy or rent. Unlike the Boomers who eagerly made the *drive till you qualify*, Millennials and Digital Natives ponder a new financial equation. The cheap housing in far-reaching suburbs is more costly when the full transportation costs are realized. Insurance, car maintenance, and filling up the tank for that long commute are a strain on the budget. These costs will continue to be an issue for younger buyers who evaluate the pros and cons of buying in more distant suburbs. An example is useful here: During the recent housing recession, properties in the outer suburbs fell far more in value, while real gas prices increased by 18 percent. The Center for Neighborhood Technology estimates that in metropolitan Washington, D.C., median home sales dropped by 41 percent in the outer suburbs but only 2 percent in the city. Meanwhile, the workers living close-in saved an estimated 21 percent on transportation costs each month. These workers may have a further advantage: their urban location affords them more career choices and flexibility, greater access to employers and higher education, and a lively social network.

There is an acronym used by planners and copyrighted by the Center for Neighborhood Technology called "H+ T." The goal is to calculate the full costs of housing plus transportation. The Washington, D.C. close-in workers spent more on housing, but they had considerable savings in transport costs. When H+T are explicit, they diminish the merit *to drive till you qualify* and signal a U-turn in policy. The next generation is reevaluating the expense, both financial and psychic, of being 100 percent car-dependent. The youngest cohort of Digital Natives has spent their youth being shuttled in school buses or household cars to sports events, after-school activities, and play dates. Now, as they make career choices, they are able to rethink the cycle. They gravitate toward locations that are more central and provide a modest transportation alternative, like a bike lane. Although they will become drivers, and acquire cars, they may never drive them as much and as far as the Baby Boomers.

CHAPTER FOUR

ALL LINKED UP: TRANSPORTATION, HOMES, & ENVIRONMENT

It's nice sitting on the patio on a warm, summer evening. But, the surroundings remind Brenda that things are not so simple. The RV uses a ton of gas...the pool pump operates eight hours a day on electricity...and the grass only stays green when the sprinklers stay on. Plus, the A/C system never seems to work as well as when they moved in. Brenda is thinking about the costs and repairs, and Elliot is still busy on his phone.

In the last chapter we introduced a transportation technology called SAVs, an acronym for "shared autonomous vehicles." There are many reasons why this innovation will be popular and forever impact our mobility. Digital Natives are more urban, and like to overlay their in-vehicle time with Internet tasks, like calling or texting. Boomers, more accustomed to getting behind the steering wheel, will find the SAVs to be particularly useful when they can no longer drive safely. A third factor propelling the technology is energy consumption. With SAVs, there are likely to be less traffic accidents, because about 40 percent of fatal crashes involve alcohol, drugs, distraction, or fatigue and an estimated 90 percent of all accidents are due to human error. Self-driving vehicles will save lives and reduce traffic bottlenecks. They are the bridge linking gray homes and a greener future.

Many Boomers now drive the Toyota Prius, and 45 percent of hybrid car owners are fifty-six years old or older (compared with electric-only vehicle owners, who are much younger). A shift from fossil fuel dependence is also occurring in the home building market. But, since houses are more permanent than carbon-belching vehicles that can be recycled in the "cash for clunkers" program, it is harder to see the mounting impact. Environmental sensibilities steer buyers away from an older, inefficient housing stock and this is not good news for Boomers who want to sell their suburban homes. Today, about four in ten homes (44%) were built before 1970 but it is often the post-1970s homes that are energy inefficient.

Most of these homes are not "energy pigs," per se. The owners have taken steps to conserve resources and manage their energy bills. Over time, they installed energy-efficient furnaces and new appliances. The problem is that these homes belong to an earlier time and space, before the Internet and before more modern building materials.

For Digital Natives, there is an opportunity to overhaul things and reduce their dependence on fossil fuels. It turns out that building homes from "ground up" is often the best energy-saving strategy. Newly built homes can take advantage of alternative energy sources like solar energy, geothermal energy, and wind power. The most important element of solar design, for example, is how the house is oriented toward the sun— many existing homes will not produce the energy efficiencies because they were not purpose-built. Short of picking up the house and reorienting it on the foundation, solar panels will fall short. That said, the energy savings from a new solar residence are substantial: a recent home that won awards from the National Association of Home Builders can produce enough surplus energy to power a car for 4,000 miles a year, and 5,000 miles farther if equipped with additional solar arrays.

Older homes, as well as many of those built between the 1970s and the 1990s, have less "innate" potential to be energy efficient. They rely on electricity and gas as fuel sources, and these fuel sources are distributed to the home by a turn-of-the last-century design, fed through a national grid. To understand how the national grid works, picture the artwork that a child would draw of a stick-figure house, and now add a garden hose going into it, and a separate garden hose leading out. Each hose is linked to a larger one at the curb, and from the curb, to a larger one at the street, and so forth. There are tremendous inefficiencies in the distribution network, and about 40% of electrical energy is said to be lost in the transmission process.

Professor Arthur Nelson says the rate of loss doubled from 20 to more than 40 percent between 1960 and 2004 because of decentralized development, that is, sprawl.

For years, phone lines, water lines, electric lines, gas lines, and cable lines were fed in a similar way. But in the last ten years utilities have become decentralized. Many Boomers have experienced this as they switched from a rotary, land-based phone to cell phone service. They may have also cut out cable TV and selected a satellite service. In the next ten to twenty years, gas and electrical service may also go "off-grid" as demand grows for more efficient, home-centered energy sources. The emergency generators home-owners purchase for backup during hurricanes and massive snowstorms are proof that they can use similar installations to power their residences more routinely.

Utilities that distribute energy from a centralized plant are not going out of business, but they are more likely to be regulated to buy energy from geothermal sources, the sun, and wind power. These energy sources will require new storage systems in homes and a digital backbone. Collectively, they spell large changes for building standards and what we consider a modern, up-to-date home. In the United States and Canada, there are few older homes still standing from the era when central heating meant wood-burning or coal-fed furnaces. Practically speaking, it has been cheaper and cleaner to tear down these obsolete homes and replace them with a different housing stock. Older homes in dense cities are the exception, probably because they are so expensive to rebuild. In the suburbs replacement homes are cheaper to build, typically less expensive to maintain, and more comfortable to live in.

Energy Dependent, by Geography

Older suburban homes are also energy pigs, solely for geographical reasons. The residents of these homes know that they need to drive everywhere—that is obvious. Less obvious is that the far-flung homes built from the 1970s onward must be serviced by a wide fleet of vehicles—typically large, energy-hungry ones—to collect trash, deliver packages, and so on. Recognizing how enormous this problem was, Amazon once proposed that convenience stores like 7-11 serve as a "pick up" spot for packages and United Parcel Service is said to be launching a similar service. Convenience stores, dry cleaners and pharmacies serve as a stop-off/pick-up point for commuters. That now seems like a small innovation, vis-a-vis some futuristic delivery by drones, but it conceptually reveals the hidden costs to service the energy-intensive suburban house.

The underbelly of suburban development is that it is difficult and energy inefficient to service the property unless an adult chooses to stay home all day. A work-around has been to install the equivalent of the modern icebox, an outdoor, key-operated storage shed with refrigeration for groceries. Suburban homes do not exactly require a servant class to feed the furnaces 24/7 or light the oil lamps twice a day. Nonetheless, suburban homes have built-in dependencies with their reliance on outside services and multiple vehicle trips.

Going forward, The Digital Natives are questioning these dependencies; they seem less patient to wait at home for the doorbell to ring, as jobs are scarce and there are better things to do with their free time. This is the cohort that earnestly supports policies to promote energy conservation and reduce carbon emissions. When polled, they are more likely than Boomers to approve federal spending on wind, solar, and hydrogen technology. This generation is less likely to buy an "Ozzie and Harriet" home that does not suit modern conventions.

Greener Boomers?

Like the Digital Natives, most Boomers pride themselves on being progressive when it comes to the environment. But many forget to include their extensive travel in the environmental report card. A German researcher who calculated carbon dioxide emissions by age group found that Baby Boomers were the highest polluters. It was not that their hearts were not in the right place, but their large homes and extensive travel, by plane and car, produced more carbon emissions. The good news is that the Boomer cohort is reducing their carbon footprint as their kids move out, and their households use less electric utilities and water.

Assuming for the moment that the Boomers stay put, can their suburban homes be retrofitted to be more environmentally sound? The likely answer is yes, assuming they have the resources and appetite for more home improvement. Boomers can continue to modify their homes and make energy efficient choices. The little inserts that come with utility bills encourage homeowners to upgrade their appliances, insulate their walls, install fans, and use LED lighting. These are not insignificant upgrades: the Department of Energy estimates that the average household energy consumption dropped by 31 percent between 1978 and 2005, while home electronics and home sizes were growing.

That said, younger homeowners are coming to view suburban homes with a different ideology. A house that is dependent solely on the grid will seem like a bad investment and an anachronism. Older buildings that devour precious energy but waste half of it through the transmission process will seem as morally wrong as deliberately burning trees to increase carbon emissions or putting ricin poison in public drinking water. And, choosing to wait at home for the delivery or repair person will seem like a dependency inherited from an earlier generation.

The implications are sobering for the suburban housing stock. The large homes that Boomers have loved and cherished may come under further threat as architects and builders shift toward a housing infrastructure that is more nimble, energy savvy, and green. The market will deem that older homes, the "energy pigs," are less desirable than smaller, closer-in places. Older homes will get torn down when it is more affordable and efficient to rebuild. Recent engineering favors homes with modular, pre-assembled components. They can be built within a couple of weeks, avoiding the environmental impacts of bringing multiple trucks, over weeks and months, to a construction site. Developers boast that their modular structures are healthier to live in, circulate air better, and protect against allergens and mold. They look nothing like the mobile, modular homes of the past.

Public policy is catching up to this environmental ethos. Curbing suburban sprawl is the intention of ongoing legislation like Senate Bill (SB) 375 in California. That celebrated 2008 bill has influenced policy in others states, as it attempts to control sprawl, rebuild cities, and create more compact and walkable communities. A key component, both in urban areas and small cities, is to ensure that there are easily accessed transportation alternatives. The spirit of the legislation favors increased density for existing development, multi-family units, and better public transportation. It reflects a U-turn for urban planners who favored single-use zoning through the 1990s. There is a rethink: the *drive till you qualify* pushed the suburbs farther out and intensified urban sprawl. This intensified energy consumption and the housing stock that once seemed so modern is looking dated and inefficient. As urban areas and transportation seem to be greening up, the SAV, the driverless car, may be the bridge between what exists today and what will emerge.

CHAPTER FIVE
GRAY HOUSE: BOOMER CASH OUT?

Now Brenda gets serious: Over their long marriage, they have bought the RV, acquired this house, and made many home improvements. It would have been nice if their kids had stayed in the area, or even moved in with them. But, it did not happen. Brenda hopes that the kid's playroom, the granite countertops, and the outdoor pool will be special to the next buyer. She stops her train of thought.... "Next buyer?" she reflects.... "Can they find one?" and, "At what price?"

The suburbs have created multiple problems for Baby Boomers. They need to plan their mobility when they can no longer drive safely, they need to maintain these large homes, and of course, at some point they may need to sell them. In this chapter we hone in on these issues, particularly the financial ones.

The cohort that preceded the Boomers, dubbed the Silent Generation, were less likely to sprawl, and they have had less difficulty hanging up the car keys as they age. This generation was also coached to save for their retirement. Even if they fell short of their financial goals, the conventional wisdom was that they could scrape by in retirement if their mortgage was paid off. Being free of debt would offset the loss of a monthly salary. Today, that wisdom does not fly; one of the most startling trends is the number of people who still have mortgages as they age. In 1989, just 37 percent of those between the ages of fifty-five and sixty-four held mortgages but in 2010 it was 54 percent. This front-wave of Boomers have traded up to larger homes, refinanced, or taken out home equity loans. But, the Boomers are not alone. Even the Silent Generation loaded up with debt and they have an important story for Boomers. Things went badly for these older retirees during the housing recession as they counted on their homes to be an "ATM".

As they enter retirement many Boomers will have to manage their debt. Before the housing crash, postponing debt management may have seemed plausible. Boomers were generating, on paper, such large capital gains from their homes that they did not feel the need to save. They expected to consume today and cash out later. John Talbott, a sage financial pundit who predicted the housing crash, says this was rational consumption: products were sold to U.S. consumers at incredibly favorable prices and manufactured overseas at incredibly low wages. Boomers anticipated that after this collective shopping spree their homes could be flipped (cashed out) to fund their medical and retirement needs. Today, Boomers have indeed cut back on their consumption. But they cannot make the price of their homes rise unless they are fortuitously located in urban areas with a growing job market, good public transportation, and bike lanes. As of December 2011 an estimated 17 percent of older households were left with houses worth less than what they owed on their home loans. The AARP estimates that about 1.5 million people age 50-plus lost their homes in foreclosure and at least 3.5 million more remain at risk.

In this chapter, we consider two financial scenarios. The first, a strategy preferred by most, is "home sweet home." Polls by the AARP indicate that three-quarters of Boomers plan to age in their homes. When people age in place, they may still need to tap the equity in their homes. It may be to offset living expenses and rising property taxes. Or, regrettably, it may be to pay the bills for nursing and health care. Whether for living expenses or medical needs, these Boomers will need to investigate the pros and cons of a reverse mortgage. The reverse mortgage, which we describe shortly, is the financial tool that spelled doom for many members of the Silent Generation during the housing recession.

The alternative scenario is to "cash out," then either rent or purchase a more suitable property, or move in with others. About 25 percent of near-retirees say they plan to sell and move, according to the AARP. Before the 2007 housing crash the oldest group of Boomers were relocating to smaller properties in warmer, mid-sized cities that had transit and walkable neighborhoods. These relocations tanked after the 2007 crash, and a recent study found that Baby Boomers showed little inclination to leave behind their single-family, detached homes.

The good news for Boomers is that the high cost of retirement may have been "oversold" to them. Kotlikoff and Burns (2012) make a compelling case that the savings guidelines have been ratcheted up by self-serving financial planners. The industry recommends that investments, housing income, and pensions add up to 70 to 85 percent of the pre-retirement income. That amount may be overstated—retirees pay significantly less for expenses like tuition, travel, and transportation. The flip side is that there are recent upticks in medical expenses and long-term health care costs. The financial planners also assume that retirees are not carrying a hefty load of mortgage and credit card debt. In fact, there has been a large increase in delinquency rates for senior borrowers. Baby Boomers are the first generation to enter retirement with substantial credit card debt.

Stay-at-Home Financing: Reverse Mortgages

Although many seniors have vowed to never again become entangled with the mortgage market, they may be pulled back into it unwittingly. One familiar and money-wise option is to refinance a mortgage at lower interest rates. New retirees may be surprised when they are turned down, even though they have substantial assets in retirement accounts or savings. Banks have traditional lending rules, and old-fashioned underwriting can disqualify wealthier retirees. For these particular retirees, a rejection will mean higher monthly expenses.

But, for the majority of retirees there will be a mortgage product that is less familiar and more onerous. Formally known as the home equity conversion mortgage (HECM or "heck-um"), it is also called the reverse mortgage. To qualify for a reverse mortgage, you need to be age sixty-two or older, own your house, and live in it full time. If you have an existing mortgage, and most Baby Boomers do, they can still qualify if there is sufficient equity to pay it off.

Between 2000 and 2007, when Boomers were trading up, refinancing, or acquiring home equity lines of credit, older seniors from the Silent Generation were lured by reverse mortgages. They were able to participate in the real-estate frenzy by cashing out. Their reverse mortgages must have initially seemed like a windfall. The seniors could choose to receive either a large single one-time payout, or an ongoing monthly stipend. Either way, the money they borrowed accrued interest costs, and the longer they stayed in their homes the more they owed on the loan when they moved or died. On paper this seemed clear, but in practice there were sinkholes.

The very word "reverse" evokes negative connotations, like the sinkhole. Seniors are not supposed to lose their homes with a reverse mortgage, but many did. They fell behind on property taxes and insurance, and their lenders took over. Other seniors neglected or could not afford basic repairs. Their properties were then worth less than their loans. When they needed to move out, say to a nursing home, they had spent their cash-out and had no savings left for the next stage of their lives.

Like other financial institutions, lenders did not anticipate the housing bubble of 2007 and the size of the market losses. The reverse mortgage is known as a "nonrecourse" loan so the government had to step in. When the loan exceeded the home's value, the lender was not allowed to collect the debt from the estate or other assets. Lenders like to point out that seniors were required by the Department of Housing and Urban Development (HUD) to undergo mandatory financial counseling. Despite counseling, most seniors elected a lump sum payment, probably to meet their basic living expenses and pay off debts. The AARP and legal counselors have weighed in with a third opinion about the pitfalls of reverse mortgages. They observe that many seniors were victimized; they did not understand the rules of this complex financial transaction. Among the hitches were excessive fees and closing costs, baiting seniors to flip the cash windfall into risky investments, and identity theft.

In Florida, and other places with senior communities, neither the borrower nor lenders took account of increasing property taxes and escalating condominium or homeowner's association fees. The seniors who took reverse loans did not budget for these reoccurring expenses. Psychologically or fiscally, they behaved as if they no longer owned the property. The state government in Florida has recently instituted a forgivable loan for reverse-mortgage homeowners.

Another vexing problem concerns ownership and title. When the senior who took out the reverse mortgage died, there were complicated legal issues for the surviving spouse or partner. Unless the spouse or partner was listed on the original document in legally binding ways, he or she could not continue to live on the property. This problem is built into the eligibility requirements since the cash-out is linked to the age of the borrower. When a younger spouse or partner is listed on the signing documents, the reverse mortgage yields a small payoff.

Meanwhile, reverse mortgages can be a minefield for younger trustees and heirs. When the owner of the property dies, or moves out, say to a nursing home, the lending institution calls in its loan. The amount that's due to the lender is the lesser of the reverse mortgage loan balance or 95 percent of the appraised value of the home. Typically the house is sold. Then, the borrower or heirs receive whatever is left, if anything. Children and caretakers are stunned if the reverse mortgage is insufficient to pay for continuing medical care or if the family homestead reverts to the bank, leaving them without an inheritance.

Reverse Mortgages Blow Up, Like Balloons

A traditional mortgage begins like a filled balloon that loses air and grows smaller each time you make a payment. The reverse mortgage has been described as an empty balloon; the amount owed on the house fills the balloon the longer the homeowner stays in the house. This may help explain the following calculations, which were derived from a reverse calculator tool, found online. Based on a 5 percent fixed interest rate or 2.5 percent floating rate, an eighty-five-year-old with a home valued at $250,000 might receive a lump sum of $97,000. Or, instead, he or she could elect a monthly payment of $1,400 (note: they have to choose between these two options). A sixty-five-year-old would receive about half of the lump sum, or could opt for a monthly payment of $734. The interest they owed on the loan would continue to grow the longer they lived in the house, and floating rates would fluctuate with the prevailing market.

Before the housing recession, reverse mortgage terms were far more favorable, and seniors (mostly the Silent Generation) could count on larger monthly balances. But the defaults were so rampant that in 2013 the government had to tighten up reverse mortgage lending and make the rules more transparent. In 2013 the U.S. Congress appropriated $1.7 billion to cover reverse mortgages gone bad. Congress also made reverse mortgages more restrictive by reducing borrowing limits and increasing insurance premiums and fees. "Round Two" of HECM have larger set-asides to ensure that property taxes, insurance, and association fees are paid.

Reverse mortgages are posed to make a comeback as Boomers investigate their remaining real estate options. Boomers who enter retirement with little savings are likely to float the boat, at least temporarily. It is important that the Boomers budget for taxes, maintenance, and insurance. And they need to recognize that payments may be fixed, but inflation levels are not. The Consumer Financial Protection Bureau has warned Congress that younger borrowers are increasingly using reverse mortgages to pay off debt, even before they retire. Down the road, these Boomers may lose their homes and be unable to recover enough savings for health care, having spent their HECM windfall.

Reverse Mortgage as Investment Strategy

Using the reverse mortgage as a financial instrument is

not straightforward. For sophisticated investors, particularly younger ones, a reverse mortgage can be used without betting the whole house. Imagine a homeowner who had different fund sources for retirement, then tapped a portion of the reverse mortgage when other investments dipped in value. For example, if a portfolio of dividend-bearing stocks tanked, then a line of credit secured from the reverse mortgage could be used to replace the expected dividend stream, assuming the market recovered. According to Kiplinger, computer simulations using this funding scenario show that the reverse mortgage strategy has a 78 percent chance of lasting thirty years, compared with a 52 percent chance for portfolios that omit it. In these models, the reverse mortgage is used as a line of credit, not withdrawn as a lump sum. When other investments drop in value, say the stock market or short-term bonds, a portion of the reverse mortgage can be tapped. After the fine print and the set-up fees, it is clear that this works better for the more sophisticated investor.

The Other Alternative: Selling the House

The more conventional option for Boomers is to sell their property, pay off the existing mortgage, and relocate. Should Boomers sell or hold out until the real estate market further recovers? That decision obviously varies with local markets and local property characteristics. A financial planner would argue that a reverse mortgage and a house sale are not that different. In both cases, the windfall (or trickle) of cash must be invested for the future or used to pay off debts.

The decision to sell is monumental because so many Boomers have not saved well; they expected to "retire on the house." A public policy professor has estimated that home equity represents 80 percent of the total wealth for about one-quarter of the older Boomers. More and more homes will be coming on the market as Baby Boomers need to unwind their holdings. People age fifty and over own close to 60 percent of the owner-occupied homes in the United States. Even if the housing market were to fully recover, their suburban homes with leafy front lawns would not be the first to sell.

As we discussed in Chapter Three, younger people are favoring urban locations with greater walkability and proximity to mass transit. Outside of urban areas, there is a marked preference for compact developments in the denser parts of suburban locations, nearer to public transit. Communities outside New York City are rezoning for multi-use, transit-oriented development; census counts from the popular suburbs of Westchester, Suffolk, and Nassau counties show declines in the number of twenty-five- to forty-four-year-olds. These changes in housing preferences are more than superficial; they spring from socio-demographic shifts toward less traditional families and smaller, one- or two-person households.

The recent economy accelerated these socio-demographic trends. When the housing market crashed, the cohort most likely to be in debt was Generation X, those born between the late 1960s and the early 1980s. This group, which was not wealthy to begin with, has seen its median incomes fall—its incomes are now lower than those of similarly aged households in 1971.

There will be knock-on effects for the Baby Boomers as younger generations are less able and less willing to re-enter the housing market. It will take the Generation X homeowners a long time to recover their assets. They may be wary of assuming additional debt as many are still saddled with student loans. With a weakening financial outlook from Generation X there will be more vacant suburban properties.

Among the younger cohort, the Digital Natives, there may be an upcoming "sea change." This is a racially mixed generation, and many have grown up in single-parent and immigrant households. They may not view home ownership as the American dream. Not surprisingly, the number of Americans in their late twenties and early thirties buying homes has slipped significantly. Only 9 percent of twenty-nine to thirty-four-year-olds got a first-time mortgage between 2009 and 2011, down from 17 percent a decade earlier. The

National Association of Realtors provides some sobering facts about the younger buyers: Generation X had a median down payment of 8 percent; for those younger, it was only 5 percent.

Renting may become the new norm for the next generation. Renting provides greater flexibility and less upfront cost, and it seems to be more tuned into cultural trends. From an economic standpoint, it means that younger age groups cannot meet the down payments and income qualifications for a new mortgage. Its members are questioning whether they want a lifestyle built around the need to service these mortgages.

A "demographic crossroad" is the way that a Forbes editor, Leigh Gallagher, who wrote a book on suburbia, puts it:

"With 61 percent of households now filled with just one or two people—and when the two largest demographic bulges—aging boomers and millennials are childless and attracted to more urban lifestyles where they don't need to drive, our traditional pattern of development isn't going to do the trick. "

Sales information from the National Association of Realtors supports this "sea change." They observe that the percentage of single female home buyers/sellers is about 4 percent among Millennials and 17 percent among Boomers and those older. The realtors' surmise that these market dynamics are driven by death and divorce.

Suburban Homes at Policy Crossroads

As if the demographic crossroads were not sufficient, there are policy turn-arounds that may further restrain the price recovery of suburban homes. As Boomers leave the workplace and their influence fades in accounting, financial, and political arenas, "favored policies" may begin to crack.

One federal policy that helps homeowners is the income tax deduction for mortgages and debt on first and even second homes. It is estimated that 20 to 30 percent of the value of a home depends on the homeowner's ability to deduct interest expense against his or her income taxes. And, some policy pundits believe the mortgage tax deduction accelerated the 2007 housing recession by encouraging many, like the Boomers, to borrow as much as possible. Other countries, including Canada and the United Kingdom, do not provide a mortgage tax deduction. As the number of renters in this country increases, there is likely to be a policy blow-back. The current tax deduction clearly favors landlords and a high home-ownership rate.

The next wave of lobbyists may promote tax deductions for homeowners and renters who display different virtues. There might be deductions for households that own just one vehicle, say a hybrid, or perhaps homeowners who install wind-powered generators. Getting a tax deduction for owning a property may be seen as a favored status in the annals of public policy. This would not favor Boomers, who have extensive mortgages and energy-inefficient homes.

Another policy U-turn is the increasing housing stock, particularly in urban areas and suburban downtowns. Zoning restrictions that guided development over the past 25 years are being thrown out. There are revisions that now encourage higher-density construction—particularly apartments and multi-family homes near transit lines. As mentioned in the chapter on energy, laws similar to California Senate Bill 375 (SB 375) are used to encourage development that promotes public transportation use, contain urban sprawl, and reduce car dependence. In practical terms, mixed-use development is favored over single-use zoning, and higher-density developments are given priority, particularly if they include a public transportation component. For Baby Boomers, this re-urbanization has consequences, since an infill of new apartment buildings would lower the sales price of suburban homes.

We noted earlier in Chapter Two that Boomers have had a mixed relationship with real estate. Now, in the final chapter of their buying, selling, and refinancing it does not appear to be getting any easier. In places to which Boomers want to move, like smaller cities with good transportation, there will be a sellers' market. In places they want to move from, there will be a buyers' market.

CHAPTER FIVE— PART II
THE COST OF MOVING ON

We have just considered the income side of the equation—how Boomers can use the equity in their homes to either age in place or to sell and move on. Although this is not a book on financial planning, it is useful to put some numbers on the cost of moving on. There may be a rude awakening: buying into a desirable retirement community, a small but well-fitted urban home, or, less fortunately, into assisted living facilities carries a big price tag.

We look at the average costs for alternative properties or living situations. Using the Internet to gauge prices, we examine several diverse living arrangements.

By way of full disclosure, these are not endorsements of particular web sites; also, the rates are dynamic, and will change, but mostly upward. The following quote, from *Forbes* magazine, sets the tone:

"The real measure of your wealth is how much you would be worth if you lost all your money" (Forbes).

1. Moving to a Smaller House in the United States (www.movoto.com/statistics)

"Cashing out" a large house for a smaller one may be the most viable financial strategy for many Boomers. Although they may not realize the full value they hoped for, they can find a more modest house or condo.

Table 5: The High Cost of Moving Elsewhere

	April 2015 median list price (movoto.com)	Median house size (square feet)	Median price ($ per square foot)
Las Vegas, Nevada	$195,900	1,726	$112
Charlotte, North Carolina	$229,900	2,025	$111.
Sarasota, Florida	$379,900	2,503	$141.
Tucson, Arizona	$196,900	1,799	$112.
San Diego, California	$529,000	1,470	$360.

Boomers should take note that smaller homes do not necessarily cost less. A recent trend in new home building has been to downsize home size but upgrade the finishes and add architectural smart design. According to the *Wall St. Journal* these new homes have small lots but upscale amenities, and they may be turning the tide. Luxury in American homes has long been defined by size (chapter one), but luxe finishes, green building and smart design are said to be taking over. The cost per square foot may reach $800 or more and rival the cost of building any McMansion.

2. Moving to a Retirement Community

(www.seniorhomes.com)

Retirement communities are housing developments marketed to people over age fifty-five. Residents live in conventional homes, typically smaller, or in an apartment or condo complex. A private firm usually manages these communities. They provide hospitality services such as dining, housekeeping, wellness programs, and activities. The firms usually have a twenty-four-hour staff on call for medical emergencies and housekeeping.

The *seniorhome*s website, which is a commercial entity, lists 144 residential communities in Arizona, but just twenty near New York City. There are other residential providers, of course. For the Arizona properties, a sampling of Tucson properties showed the minimum monthly cost to be $2,250, with two bedroom units starting at $4,695. A headline on the website asks, "Why Rent a Senior Apartment When I Already Own a Home?" The sales plugs are, "you can free up equity from the sale of a home for travel and investment, trade home maintenance chores and yard work for leisure activities and come and go without worrying about the home...and have a greater sense of security than living in a private home."

3. Assisted Living
(www.seniorhomes.com/p/assisted-living-cost)

Like residential real estate, assisted living costs will vary due to geographical location and local wages. Other factors that determine the monthly cost are the level of care provided, the size of the domicile, and any special needs. The care of dementia patients, for example, requires skilled nursing and is far more expensive than assisted living.

According to Metropolitan Life Insurance (MetLife) the national average for assisted living base rates was $3,550 per month in 2012. There have been 3 to 5 percent annual increases.

The website listed above has a useful chart which shows the range of monthly assisted living costs, state by state, in 2013 for a one-bedroom, single-occupancy apartment. The lowest rate is $718 a month in Michigan and the highest is $9,500 a month in New York City.

4. Stay at Home: The Villages Model

(www.vtvnetwork.org)

For Boomers wishing to age in place, it may take a village. The village model started fifteen years ago with a nonprofit in Boston called "Beacon Hill Village." It was organized as an individualized, grassroots solution to aging in place. Seniors continue to age in place, in their own homes but have a support network to call on. The support network might range from group outings and exercise clubs to finding vetted, in-home helpers. The support network is run by a combination of volunteers and paid employees but they are also tapped into social service programs for the aging.

Today, there are at least eighty villages in the United States, and they vary greatly by size and services. Based on a 2012 study done by Rutgers University, the average fees for an individual membership are $430 and $586 per household. Households pay an annual membership fee, which is often income adjusted. In return they are linked into a network of preferred providers, for needs ranging from medicine to transportation to computer classes. One of the most requested services is said to be for handyman to help maintain large, older homes.

An acronym, called NORC, is used to describe Naturally Occurring Retirement Communities. NORC communities are regular homes that are geographically proximate and happen to have more retirees. The original Village, in Boston, was a NORC. Clusters of

NORCS will happen organically as the Millennials leave the suburbs and Boomers stay in place.

5. Home Exchanges and Shared Living

Home exchanges and shared living are old concepts finding new traction in the current economy. They are useful as people make big plans for retirement without big budgets. With shared living, households are consolidated, and like-minded people share a common residence or compound. There are many variations on this: one of the happier descriptions is the "Golden Girls" story of three single Baby Boomer women who retired together in Mt. Lebanon, Pennsylvania. They wrote a book popular book titled, appropriately, *"My House, Our House: Living Far Better for Far Less in a Cooperative Household."*

A second model does not involve a change in residence per se, but it enables Boomers to make more use of their properties. Home exchanges, generally arranged over the Internet on sites *seniorshomeexchange.com* and *homelink.org* enable Boomers who are healthy and adventurous to travel without incurring the additional expenses of lodging and eating out.

A third take on aging in place is to stay put but rent out the extra rooms, possibly in exchange for driving. This may hark back to an earlier time. Social historians estimate that between a third and half of 19th century urban residents were either boarders themselves, or took boarders into their homes. It is likely that the Boomer's grandparents or great-grandparents lived in a "multi-tenant" household.

6. Move Out of the Country

Although most retirees stay in the United States, moving overseas is a viable alternative. The cost of living can be much lower and the standard of living can be higher. International Living, a magazine and website, provides a comparison of locations. There are also popular books on the topic, and they go over the basics like taxes, health care, safety, social security, and doing a "test run."

Two popular retirement venues are Mexico and Costa Rica. There are approximately 50,000 retirees in Costa Rica, and the attraction, according to *Marketwatch*, is that they can enroll in the country's public health system. In Mexico, which has an estimated 40,000 to 80,000 U.S. retirees, the AARP estimates that mid-price condos and houses near Puerto Vallarta will cost $200,000, beach front villas cost $300,000 and up, and year-round rentals start at $800 a month. They add that bargains can be found.

No one knows exactly how many people have opted to retire overseas, but about 350,000 Americans receive social security benefits in countries outside the U.S. according to the Social Security Administration's annual supplement.

CHAPTER SIX

GRAY HOMES: SHRINKING THE KIDS

Brenda is both serious and engaged- it's not just about the money. They bought this house after their second child was born. It had plenty of space, and there was room for everyone. But, now it's just too big too manage. When the kids visit at Christmas, it's too cold to use the pool. When they travel to the kids, it's a pain to close up the house and have a worry-free vacation.

In the last chapter we described the financial meltdown. While all markets will not be impacted equally, there will be a sell-off as the Boomers wind down. At least 28 million homes, possibly many more, will go on the market. Should Boomers decide to age in place, can they count on their children and grandchildren to be their designated drivers? If they sell, will their large homes be desirable to the next generation? In this chapter we turn to more sociological issues and explore the desirability of these homes for the next generation.

As a starting point, consider that post World War II suburbs— like Levittown, New York, were best suited for a nuclear family in which one parent commuted to work and the other stayed home with children. In this Ozzie and Harriet model, other mothers were around during the day, and the neighborhood offered plenty of social activities. By the 1980s the rise of housing prices and the two-income family caused the model to unravel, and the suburbs became a lonely place, designed more for cars than people.

If you asked Boomers *why* they bought in the suburbs, the most likely answer would be that the suburbs provided a better environment for raising their children, and future grandchildren. But, did parents who spent so much time commuting overshadow the family-friendly virtues of suburban homes? And, will the Boomers grandchildren be raised well if their parents seem to always be on the road?

We will also drill down on a special case—when adult children do not move out. We hint that in some cases, adult children's "failure to launch" may be linked to Boomers' singular relationships with their homesteads. If these adult children continue to stay in place, and do not set up their own households, they may unwittingly become caretakers when their parents' health begins to decline. We proposed in Chapter One that the suburbs were "no country for old men" or old women. Here we add that they the suburbs often do not serve young people well either.

If you have difficulty picturing this, think of how high schools in suburban and rural areas serve their students. Large hulky school buses (the yellow peril) travel vast, circuitous routes and deposit students at centrally located campuses. The facilities are expansive, with taxpayer-funded amenities like running tracks, football fields, and swimming pools, but the students spend excess time in transit and must schedule their free time around the transportation schedule. Most kids would probably vote for smaller, simpler facilities if they could walk or ride bikes instead.

Children at the Center

In Dr. Seuss's *Cat in the Hat*, two children are left alone at home on a rainy windy day, and the mischievous cat sneaks in and probes "what they want to play since their mother is away." The outcome is havoc and chaos, until the children realize that they have to expel the cat and clean up before Mom gets home.

Although Boomers did not literally leave their children and grandchildren with Dr. Seuss's bad cat, figuratively they did. Their children, Millennials and Digital Natives, passed the day with an average of six hours a day of television or movies as well as hand-held video games. Neil Postman, an early media critic, called this "amusing ourselves to death." While single videos are not pernicious, their cumulative volume might be. There is an unsettling awareness that something is amiss in the neighborhood as a new class of angry, psychotic young men shoot up their hometown movie theaters and schools. On the other hand, the overall rate of petty crimes is falling, and this is attributed to teens spending so much time *inside* their homes and not on the streets.

When they first entered the housing market, Boomers were convinced that suburbia provided kids with "extras" like a big fenced yard with a swing set, or a large comfortable TV room. They did not calculate that the child with a backyard swing set was less likely to enjoy unsupervised playtime with their peers, in a park or on the streets. With a jumbo TV screen in the family room, there was less enticement to visit a movie theater, a puppet show, or a live baseball game. Individually, these were small losses, but they might add up to a bigger collective over eighteen years, from birth through high school.

Suburban homes are hardly prisons, but when the Digital Natives were young adolescents, it probably felt that way. Without a driver's license, they had limited opportunities to leave the house and explore on their own. Riding bicycles was often discouraged as it was viewed as unsafe. Even today, children growing up in the suburbs are dependent on baby-sitters, caretakers, or parents to drive them places. These children, who are driven to school, to friends' homes, and to after-school sports, learn slowly and late, to cross a street alone and to look both ways. At the end of the 1980s, there seemed to be a wake-up call and collective awareness that kids were spending too much time indoors, with one-way media. So, middle-class parents began to "program" their children's out-of-school activities like soccer and tutoring. Children participated in more live activities, but these scheduled activities multiplied the time spent in the car.

Although it is speculative, there are hints that this phase was not conducive for raising children. Children participated in more live activities, but they spent hours traveling back and forth. Now, as young adults, this generation has discovered that living in urban areas lets them claw back some of the precious time spent in the car. For modern, working, dual-income households with one or two children, living in an urban area makes child raising more social and less stressful. Parents with school-age children are less likely to relocate if urban schools improve or if options such as charter schools sprout up. Urban teens gain more freedom and parents hover over them less when they don't have to worry about safety in cars. Kids can be more sociable if friends live nearby and they can drop in at any time. Not surprisingly, a next generation of homebuyers shows a strong preference to live in more urban developments with an array of housing types close to shops and mass transit. Further down the road, their preferences may lead to more compact development in downtown suburban locations.

Looking back in twenty or thirty years, the child-centric suburban home may come to seem like an odd phase in child raising. The suburban home, with a stay-at-home mother, was an artifact or luxury of the 1950s and 1960s. By 1990, when 74 percent of women entered the workforce, the luxury eroded into a latchkey *Cat in the Hat* syndrome. Moreover, 45 percent of younger Baby Boomers, born between 1957 and 1964, had marriages ended in divorce, leaving one parent, typically the mother, to do double duty. It should not be a surprise that their progeny have a different view of child raising. Younger cohorts are having smaller families and view the suburban tract with less bliss. For Boomers who are trying to sell these properties or extract their equity it does not help that the suburbs are no longer romanticized as a child-friendly haven.

The children who grew up in these suburbs have another gripe. Since the recession, these young adults enrolled in school or extended their education. To do so, a greater number took out student loans, since their parents' home equity or household savings were tapped out. *The Wall St. Journal* reports that the delinquency among student borrowers increased after the 2007 recession, as younger people went to school to escape a weak labor market. While they have better job skills, their job prospects sometimes remain "anemic." This problem is not limited to the youngest age groups, as student debt has grown substantially among older adults in their thirties and forties. Both age groups are disadvantaged as they try to qualify for new mortgages, or negotiate pricey rental contracts.

Failure to Launch

Kim Parker, of the Pew Foundation, notes that if there's supposed to be a stigma attached to living with Mom and Dad through one's late twenties or early thirties, today's "boomerang generation" didn't get that memo. Between 2007 and 2010 the number of kids living with their parents increased by 5.2 percent for those under twenty-five, and 17.5 percent among those older. The Census notes that the trend to live at home actually began around 2005, before the recession. In the 2011 Current Population Study an estimated 19 percent of young men and 10 percent of young women, ages twenty-five to thirty-four, lived at home. Now, in the post-recession era, things have not changed that much. Close to 20 percent of the U.S. population lives in multi-generational family households and the share has continued to increase. One of the interesting twists, noted in a recent Gallup study, was that among young adults who lived at home, nearly one in five has added a spouse or partner to their parents' household!

The decision to live at home is attributed by the popular press to many factors. These include the high unemployment rate among high school and college graduates, a lack of savings for a down payment or rental, and a demographic shift to postpone the age at marriage. A less mentioned factor is that living at home provides a better standard of living for those earning a minimum wage. It is agreeable for a generation that grew up with high expectations for comfort and leisure.

While all of these factors are important and cannot be understated, they do not address the underbelly of the issue: the child-centric household Boomers once exalted. The centermost circle, in their minds, was the welfare of their children. As these children matured, Boomers did not have to "let go." With their large, empty suburban homes Boomers now have the space and resources to accommodate their adult children. The privacy of a large house coupled with ample bedrooms, and the ability to come and go with a third or fourth household vehicle, makes this living situation agreeable to all parties. Boomers, and particularly Boomer women, are accustomed to providing "gendered duty" for aging parents, and now adult children. And, it is certainly an improvement from the recent past when they chauffeured their teens.

This is a generational shift. When Boomers came of age, staying at home was less feasible, since their parents had smaller homes and these households did not own a second or third car. The societal expectation was that able kids moved out, even if it was to cramped and grubby student quarters. The Boomers, through their largess and love, have made it comfortable and clubby to stay at home. For some, the failure to launch is an advanced case of the over-reaching, over-involved, helicopter parent. Unintentionally, having adult children at home continues to justify the Boomers' need to age-in-place. The downside is that it puts in jeopardy the upward—or outward—movement of the entire family.

Individually, Boomers will not be able to sell their homes at a better price if their adult children move out.

But, collectively, the housing market would improve if adult children did relocate *en masse*. Curiously, the failure to launch has an impact on the entire housing market: when young adults move out, marry, divorce, and so forth—they establish new households. Before the 2007 recession, each new home formation rippled through the economy with purchases of homes and additional goods and services. A Pew study estimates that only about one-in-three Millennials head their own household, and that the rate has continued to fall. Moody's Analytics estimates that nearly 1.1 million new households are now missing because of the recession and current trends.

Decisions about where and when to move are never easy, but there is an added complication when the living arrangements of adult children complicate the picture. Boomers seem oblivious to the fact that as they age-in-place they may need to call on their family members to help out. If their adult children are in residence, having them *en situ* may become an "inconvenient truth." Many Boomers are not prepared for their financial future, particularly when their medical needs will increase. They will not be able to afford the assisted living and skilled nursing they require.

Most Boomers are not aware of the forthcoming clash as their health declines. Caretaking will require young adults to put family needs ahead of individual aspirations. Ironically, the Boomers have cherished values like self-actualization, personal expression, and independence.

A historian, Hendrik Hartog, has looked into the future and summed it up this way: *"The parent child bond rarely runs as strongly from child to parent as it does the other way. No one in the modern world thinks that caring for old parents is what their life's work is. At best, it's a distraction, at worst, a burden."* Down the road, the multigenerational household may become a necessity if the aging Baby Boomers decline in health but age-in-place.

Curiously, the multigenerational household can present another impediment, a financial one, when adult children live at home and fail to launch. Over time, adult children may develop a vested interest in the financial outcome of the home- the investment they stand to inherit. If Mom and Dad move out from under them, this nest-egg is placed in jeopardy.

In the financial chapter we saw how expensive it can be to relocate to retirement communities with the monthly fees that rival any large mortgage. Boomers who have nearly paid off their mortgage and do not have outstanding debts *can* afford to move. But, swapping their homes for a retirement village brings financial issues into play. These retirement villages are costly and could siphon the housing equity their kids expected to inherit. For adult children who still live at home, it is a no-win situation. First, if Mom and Dad move out, these kids would have to find someplace else to live, an expensive proposition. Second, Mom and Dad are likely to use the sale of their home, their home equity, to finance the move to a retirement community. When Mom and Dad pass away, there might be little or no property inheritance, since the retirement community "ate the house" with its monthly fees and assessments. The economic implications are not favorable for Boomers: the longer their adult children continue to live at home, the more likely these children will need to in the future, as the need and medical dependencies increase.

Rebranding Children and Community

In current real-estate markets, many urban areas are "hot" and the suburbs are lagging, unless they border a major city and have good transportation. As the desirability of the suburbs shrinks, real estate developers are seizing on family values as a way to market their next building projects. There is recognition that suburbs will become even duller, emptier places, so builders are rebranding them as "urban villages" and "lifestyle centers." Real estate developers hope that a new suburban "core" will simulate an urban village and gathering area. They envisage that the suburbs will be rejuvenated, as the core draws people of all ages from surrounding homes. Cores, the rebranded town commons, sound like a good idea, but the thinking neglects a vital factor. Unless older people can drive from their remote cul-de-sacs, safely negotiate the busy streets, and park close by, they will not participate in the commons. To some, these commons are strangely reminiscent of an older enclosed shopping center losing its second story and morphing into an all-seasons outdoor mall.

Meanwhile, new immigrants and larger families continue to move to the suburbs. A noted professor of urban studies, Joel Kotkin, expects this trend to continue. The demographic trends we saw in Chapter One underscore the importance of immigration. Kotkin also anticipates that the Millennial generation, which reflects a multi-racial demographic, will still favor suburban amenities once they settle down and have children. He says that the sprawling suburbs will continue to be favored by families seeking a better place to raise their kids. Assuming this is so, the key factor will be whether suburban schools continue to provide kids with a quality education. Over the past forty years, suburban school boards could draw on a growing tax base and special assessments. In the future, that tax base could shift. This will happen if younger, hip parents choose to locate in more urban areas, most likely neighborhoods that have smaller homes near public transportation. The erosion of the suburban tax base may already be occurring. In the last decade, the prevalence of high-poverty suburban communities—where more than 20 percent of people live below the poverty line—expanded rapidly. The full implications of the suburban "poor" have not yet been felt, but it cannot bode well for the children.

CHAPTER SEVEN

THE GAME CHANGER—BOOMERS AND TECHNOLOGY

Now the story is in Elliot's hands, literally. Seated on the porch beside her, he has not heard Brenda's question about driving the RV. His mind is elsewhere. Elliot is catching up on the texts he missed during the day, consulting his calendar, planning his fantasy football team...all on his Smart Phone.

In previous chapters we described the status quo: after World War II, Americans started producing larger families. The result, today, is nearly 75 million aging Baby Boomers, the oldest of which are now sixty-five and the youngest fifty. There was another post-war trend: mushrooming consumerism, initially led by the demand for new and used cars. As soon as they turned sixteen, Boomers lined up at motor vehicle departments to get their licenses. Later, the Boomers were willing to driver farther to live in nicer homes. The *drive till you qualify* opened up new suburbs and led to an expansionary period for housing development. Now we introduce a third dimension that upends the status quo: in this chapter we explore the reaches of new technology. If the idea in Chapter One of aging in place with the assistance of a nanny robot was a shock, Boomers should get ready for further surprises.

Both scientists and journalists use an overworked phrase called "disruptive technology" to describe a breakthrough that changes or "breaks up" the status quo. The automobile, for example, was a disruptive technology—it made obsolete the oxen that plowed fields, as well as the horse and buggy. It fueled, literally, the society we know today. Imagine if you told a farmer in 1872 that in fifty years he would be cultivating his fields with a gas-powered tractor. That invention would surpass his imagination.

Today, we are facing a mismatch between homes that people want to live in and the ones that were erected over the past century. In many ways that also surpasses our imagination. Part of the mismatch is location—older people need to drive less and younger people seem to have a preference for other transportation. There is also a growing mismatch as our culture prizes flexibility and things digital: younger people are less interested in expressing themselves through the maintenance and decoration of stationary homes. This is a shift in consumer culture. The third factor is simpler: suburban homes have grown bigger and often energy inefficient while family sizes, and budgets, are shrinking. Technology is undermining the value we ascribe to traditional homesteads.

It is hard to grasp that our beloved family homes may be "homely," but housing stock becomes as obsolete as an old car—it just takes longer. The U.S. government has a program that replaces old, substandard homes with more efficient buildings. But, to understand "obsolete," let's first take a detour to a town that has known disruptive change first hand. It is

Newport, Rhode Island. The 1974 version of *The Great Gatsby* movie was filmed there, and an even more epic saga took place within the fabled mansions. You cannot be a resident there without accepting that as time marches on, even the most exquisite properties languish and become undesirable, at least for a period of time. It happens to be the town where the author of this book grew up.

Both historians and real estate brokers from Newport are well versed in the ravages of disruptive technology. The technology of electricity is a household staple today, but at one time it was novel. It literally outdated mansions dripping in opulence. Here is the reason:

In the 1880s an elite group of wealthy individuals, who came to be called "the 400" established summer cottages in Newport. Their massive homes were commission by a new moneyed elite, largely New York industrialists. This period was called the Gilded Age, as new mansions and villas sprang up, each one more posh and decorous. Despite their outward glamour, the underpinning of these homes was a nineteenth-century infrastructure. The giant kitchens operated with ice boxes for keeping food cold, the stoves were wood burning, and a bevy of servants were responsible for lighting gas-powered chandeliers and fixtures at the beginning and end of each day, usually with whale-oil. At the end of the century the gas lamps and coal were about to be displaced by the discovery of in-ground oil. And, the new invention of electricity was soon to disrupt the standard way of building these homes.

The wealthiest owners began to wire their mansions for electricity on an experimental basis, while they retained oil lamps for backup. By 1910 many of the residences were fully retrofitted. But, even with their retrofit, the mansions were never as comfortable and easy to live in as purpose-built homes. The Newport "cottages" were hard to heat and drafty. By 1960 the quality of the original wiring was decaying and the cost of upgrading it was excessive. The mansions were dilapidated, the wiring was dangerous, the roofs were leaking, and the plumbing was inadequate. Investors looking to buy these mansions were put off by the cost of these renovations and often acquired the properties for their land-value.

Electricity, and then World War I, played a fundamental, disruptive function for Newport's upscale real estate. Electricity ushered in an age of do-it-yourselfers (DIY). The technology shut the household door on butlers, maids, and a serving staff. With a wall switch to turn the lights on and off, it was no longer necessary to have a butler bring a gas flame and "torch" the sconces in a massive house. The war contributed, and made it hard to find this laboring class. The invention of electricity made obsolete a crew of coal-soaked men working in the dank basement to shovel fuel in the furnace around the clock. Likewise, kitchen staffs that plied the cooking stoves with wood and washed and ironed clothes with hot steam were made redundant.

Sales prices for the summer cottages plummeted. Only in the 1980s, when developers discovered that they could chop these homes into condominium units and sell them off by pieces did the market rebound. Not surprisingly, the market for these properties dropped with the 2007 recession but has rebounded as wealthy new buyers, including those from the tech industry, buy up the large estates.

But Newport is not the only story of disruptive technology that frames the ups and downs, the desirability of real estate. In more contemporary times, we can trace the rise and fall of the home-video store. There are lessons in this commercial real estate for residential properties. Baby Boomers will recall that that the video store, through the 1990s, was as plentiful and popular on street corners as a Starbucks coffee shop. At one point Blockbuster was retail colossal with roughly 5,500 stores and franchises. Until 2005, it was able to keep up with an exploding technology that evolved from VHS, to CD, and finally DVD formats. And, then it crashed. According to the *Wall St. Journal,*

"The company (Blockbuster) was sold for $8 billion in stock as recently as 1994 but only $234 million in 2010. A newer disruptive technology,

streaming video, pushed it into bankruptcy. In 2011 there were only 1,700 locations and the number of stores continues to dwindle."

It is difficult for Baby Boomers to imagine that their houses in suburbia will be subject to the same disruptions as the video store! After all, they reason—if you visit the housing stock of European cities, say London or Amsterdam—these homes are at least 100 years old and have withstood the ravages of technology.

The counterpoint is that these are urban homes, in the city core. The demand has grown geometrically, and the supply of land is fixed, so urban properties are not in decline. In the United States, properties in Boston, San Francisco, and New York City escalate in value as jobs and workers relocate. Older housing stock is highly desirable in these major cities and zoning seems to further restrict building new development. The renewed interest in living in cities is an irony for Boomers, who vacated them in the 1980s to buy in new, far-away suburban tracts. Not unlike the fortunate "400" of Newport, Boomers preferred suburban tract homes that provided more space, greater luxury and upscale amenities. They also seemed to have enjoyed the muscle cars, the pick up trucks, and later on, S.U.V models, that complemented the suburban household.

In Newport, tastes changed: one hundred years ago it was fashionable to show your wealth by importing exotic marble and fine woods. The homes also had dedicated spaces for recreation and leisure, like ballrooms, billiard rooms, libraries, and an occasional conservatory or bowling alley. Most of these spaces, like the library, the bowling alley, and the ballroom, filtered into the public realm, and the activities moved to the public realm. Today, the scope is different, but the sentiment may be similar: spaces in the desirable, upscale homes of thirty years ago are becoming dated. Suburban houses that were built with big TV or family rooms and two- and three-car garages are becoming redundant as tastes and technology march on.

The differences are small, but they are growing. New media are streamed to portable devices so the big family room seems overbuilt. Occasions to watch big-screen TV are becoming more social, and take place with friends at a restaurant or sports bar. The massive two or three car garage is the most flagrant example of how space needs change. Big garages are wasteful when you downsize your auto fleet and use a mobile app to flag a quick ride.

Baby Boomers were born in the heyday of automobiles and have difficulty imagining that there are alternatives to sitting behind the steering wheel. The youngest generation does not have this affinity— they come with a different mindset. This cohort, sometimes called Digital Natives, do not know a time before the Internet. There are new innovations, brought on by the Internet, that disrupt older standards. The Digital Natives are just beginning to make their impact felt in the real estate market.

There are at least three ways the impacts will be felt: The first impact is the ability of the Internet to reshape attitudes and behavior toward travel, meetings, and the use of physical space. Communicating digitally instead of in person or by physically sending things will encourage *the death of distance.*

The second impact is about values and what we perceive to be of material importance. In an Internet economy, experience trumps possessions. It also alters what we hold dear- how we store memories, and how we respect and evaluate our friendships and relationships. Some would say the Internet hastens *the death of things material.*

The third factor leads us to rethink *how everyday things and relationships are carried out.* Baby Boomers, a socially minded cohort, extolled slogans like, "Make Love, Not War." A newer ethos places supreme confidence in innovation and technology. The younger generation is vested in technology. They trust that the likes of nanny robots will provide care for their Boomer parents and grandparents.

In the next three sections, we elaborate on each trend. We explore how the impacts will reach Baby Boomers seeking a comfortable retirement in suburbia.

The Internet: The Death of Distance

The Internet, that invisible yet ubiquitous ether of exchange, is a disruptive technology for suburban homeowners. Innovations shake up what people do in their homes, and hence, where it is desirable to live. To explain this we return to our recent example of Blockbuster stores and the video rental business.

Most Baby Boomers will fondly recall the stores that stocked movie videos. Some may have met their spouses there, as these locations were a celebrated hangout for singles. When video stores expanded through the 1980s the business model was aligned with a car-based culture. People willingly "traveled to rent" the movie entertainment. The "travel to rent" model began to look shaky when audio-sharing files emerged. The model became unglued when Netflix, and others, improved data compression and could engineer bandwidth to rapidly stream video and audio. No longer did households need to "travel to rent." The video could be more efficiently streamed to a set box, just like over-the-air TV.

The design, use, and location of suburban and rural homes are now under pressure from the Internet, but like the Blockbuster chain, the impact may not be seen for a few years, perhaps a decade. When the impact is fully realized, there will be such dramatic shifts that Boomers will be surprised they did not see it coming. Geographical preference has already played out for Blockbuster—the old storefronts stand vacant, or have been repurposed into Starbucks or Petco stores.

As of 2014, change seems far off. If anything, the Internet seems to be creating a better functioning suburban home, letting its inhabitants shop less at stores, ordering both the mundane and the unique over the Internet. Electronic "papyrus"—newspapers, books, and tutoring services—can be streamed to the house. These digital services allow households to "cocoon" if they wish—to travel less and still "intake" the same level of products and services, perhaps even more. Our newly wired homes are serviced almost daily by the postal service as well as a growing fleet of brown UPS trucks and purple FedEx vehicles. In many ways, this could help older people who have less mobility, as groceries and toilet paper arrive on their doorstep.

In the short run, older people must learn to use smart phones and order online. That is manageable. The bigger problem, over a longer run, is that this new paradigm does not bring people face to face. Since the beginning of time, people have gathered in the marketplace; the modern mall is the latest incarnation of a long tradition. The physical need for these centers is fading with Amazon purchases, but the social need remains strong or stronger. This may be one of the reasons that younger people are shunning the suburbs for more urban settings. Like a drone on the horizon, the change is imperceptible now, but headed our way. Not only have the video stores closed, but so have the travel agents, the book stores, small appliance sales and service centers, and others—all being pushed aside by an Internet economy. Commercial enclaves that serviced the suburban and rural stores are being eroded by newly efficient one-click shopping and home delivery. The economy is changing but people are not. As the suburban landscape morphs, people still seek out gathering points. Younger people, on the brink of the upheaval, are choosing to live in closer proximity to each other and socialize in person.

The closing of these local stores, and their evolution into a different form, is disruptive. It does not spell good outcomes for aging, long-time suburban owners. If there are fewer retail outlets, suburban homes will become more like geographic islands. Healthy, able home owners will need to drive farther, in more traffic, to reach quality stores and services in more centralized locations.

For Boomers who want to age in place, there is an assumption (since there is no elder school bus, but there is Dial-A-Ride) that things will stay the same. Boomers expect that the local food market, perhaps a five-mile drive away, will remain open and the knowledgeable guy at the local hardware store, maybe a block or two from the supermarket, will be around, too. And, the expectation is that other businesses—the corner bookstore that hosts a monthly book reading, the country store that sells fertilizers and seasonal Christmas trees, and so forth—will stay fixed. In the suburban mind, everything is staying the same, despite the daily influx of those large brown- and purple-colored delivery fleets. The commercial landscape is shifting, but like the Blockbuster stores that closed down, the pace is initially slow and then it's over.

When the disruptive technology of the Internet does come to pass and its impact is more fully realized, older people who have stayed in their homes will be more socially isolated, more dependent on their computers for daily tasks, and more needy for transportation. It is an insidious process: the more we use the Internet and enjoy what it brings into our homes, the more it will disrupt the desirability of these homes. The digital economy is growing and it will give future homeowner's a new set of ideas and preferences. The homes we currently live in are fixed to an earlier style and technology, and becoming outdated.

The Internet: The Death of "Things" Material

Despite the fact that we buy more things on the Internet and fewer things in brick-and-mortar stores, the overall rate of spending in the United States is not rising. In fact, another disruptive trend is taking place. Younger people are downsizing and discarding the material trappings of conspicuous consumption. The Internet is a strong impetus of change, as experience, novelty, and agility trump solid, staid, and secured.

Boomers, at face value, are resistant to this transformation. They are likely to see as a passing fancy the youthful opinion expressed by a twenty-something in this *New York Times* article. Robert Rhinehart, inventor of a food replacement product described how he reexamined consumerism. He saw a parallel between the sport of hiking and his everyday quality-of-life, *"You want to be aggressively minimal, to get the volume and mass of everything as low as possible. Then I started to do the same thing in my normal life... actually, it seemed that the harder something was to get rid of, the more cleansing it was to do it."*

Boomers may have trouble swallowing the minimalism since they bought such large houses and filled them with "stuff." A minimalism perspective is more likely to resonate if they have also traveled a lot, or recently rented or leased a property with Airbnb, which stands for "air bed and board." It is easier to rent out your house or apartment, and experience a vacation in someone else's home, if there are fewer personal possessions to worry about and fewer valuables that can be broken or mishandled. Possessions are extra baggage in an Internet culture. Airbnb, an entirely new business model, personifies how values shift from material possessions to experience. Bragging rights are less in the acquisition of items, and more in the information and pictures we post online.

At an earlier time, before global manufacturing and the Internet, it was valuable to hand stuff down, generation to generation, and to cherish, both physically and emotionally, these attachments. Manufacturing was a hard-scrapple process, and replacement costs were relatively dear. The Internet

Age, and possibly the 3-D printer, turn this equation upside down and make stuff a "commodity" to be replaced.

If it difficult to imagine that this trend is a keeper—that it is here to stay—let's return to Newport, Rhode Island, and imagine a Boomer's house filled with Victorian and English antiques. In the 1970s the market for these items was expanding, and a small collection—say of a dining room table and chairs, a buffet, and a nicely carved bed—might have been worth $4,000 to $6,000. The rational was that antiques are scarce, they are not making any more of them (reproductions exempted), and they can only increase in value. In 1980, these same seven pieces might have reached a peak value at auction of about $7,000 to $10,000, according to the Antiques Reference Database. Today, major auction houses would refuse the items, since they would sell for a pittance. Tastes have simply changed.

As their wealth increased between the nineteen nineties and 2007, Boomers were happy consumers. When their spare bedrooms, basements, and garages could be stuffed no further they found another solution, the self-storage unit. With their large SUVs and mini-vans, they went off-site. The self-storage industry ballooned along with the Boomers' 2000–2007 buying spree. It took the self-storage industry more than twenty-five years to build its first billion square feet of space; it added the second billion square feet in just eight years, between 1998 and 2005. The industry estimates that one in six Americans uses off-site storage.

The stuffed storage sheds reflect countless shopping trips and many individual purchasing decisions. But, as television viewers of the scripted TV show *Storage Wars* know, and as real-life owners can attest, most of the stuff in these sheds is useless. This is an acute problem for Boomers who need to downsize and move to smaller residences or medical facilities, and for those who plan to stay in place. The majority of their "stuff" will have no real monetary value, but will be emotionally difficult to part with. Again, there will be exceptions. But, for every ten *Antique Roadshow* winners, there will be ten thousand no-starters.

The replacement society suits the Millennial generation, and the younger cohorts, known as Digital Natives. Imagine the ease of furnishing an apartment or house over a weekend by shopping either in person or online at Ikea, the Swedish hypermarket. Ikea provides simplicity and chicness—albeit, with assembly required. Should you need to move again—suppose you landed a better job or your household partners changed—you could be agile. Ikea has seen this opportunity, and is marketing directly to the next generation of Digital Natives. The most recent business plan heralds Internet marketing in lieu of building more Ikea showrooms.

The Internet is enabling this fluid, agile economy along with a related method to shed material possessions. It is known as the Share Economy and since 2008 it has grown exponentially. Like Airbnb, the Internet brings a rethinking of old customs, particularly for sharing things. It used to be cumbersome to share items that you needed now and then, but not often, say a twelve-foot extension ladder to clean the gutters or a fourteen-piece dinner setting used for a Thanksgiving dinner with friends. There were rental stores, like United Rentals, that provided these items, but usually to a niche market. Today, share is becoming mainstream, and there is no need for these storefronts. In Europe, the share economy is taking off in a big way, and companies are trying to control the market so they don't lose consumers. Before the Internet, it was difficult to bring people together to ignite a share economy. Now it is becoming a new way to bring together people and possessions.

Ironically, one of the first share prototypes was for automobiles. Car share began nearly forty years ago in Europe, often at train stations. Today there are an estimated 800,000 car sharing members in the United States and 1.7 people million worldwide. Sharing cars has become a market reality that promises to reduce urban congestion, parking, and the cost of vehicle ownership. One of the key reasons it works is efficiency: the average car is parked and idle for 95 percent of the day.

The Internet cannot be kind, over the long run, to traditional firms like the big moving companies, storage shed owners, and the middling antique market. These are the very businesses that the Baby Boomers helped grow. Now, mobility comes to trump possessions, and the more possessions we carry forward, the more burdened and slowly we move. This is a sea change for Baby Boomers, who have been weaned since birth on a gluttonous path of consumption. Just a decade ago, it was a trendy thing to boast that you and your offspring were "born to shop."

But, those cutesy born-to-shop stores seem to be closing; exercise facilities and yoga studios are sprouting up instead. Yoga exemplifies a new economy: the practice requires, at most, a small mat. Fancy spandex tops do not improve the quality of the practice (although stylish studios might try to sell us otherwise). The greatest expenses to open a studio are the shiny, polished floor and the tranquil, high-efficiency lighting. The ambience is achieved with less furniture, less decoration, and, certainly, less start-up cost.

This design ethos will be copied in homes; simple furniture will be desirable if it can be used multi-purposely, a style honed in Japan. Boomers' households that are tricked out from the likes of Ethan Allen and Home Goods may come to seem as cluttered and superfluous as the stuffy Edwardian living rooms decorated with antimacassars (covers) on the velvet chesterfield (sofa). Marching toward Goodwill stores are big chesty armoires from the media rooms, frumpy wood rockers, and Adirondack chairs.

Still, the trend to scale back will harbor new forms of consumerism and different ways to shop. For example, during the 2007–2009 economy, marketing experts watched an old category take on new importance. With fewer children, both Millennials and Boomers spent more on their pets. During the recession, the sales growth of pet products slowed, but still had growth, which was not the case for most other industries.

Jumping from pets to homes is a big leap, but marketers are taking stock of Millennials' changing tastes. According to a recent real estate survey of a thousand adults, ages eighteen to thirty-five, smaller, functional homes are preferred over sprawling

McMansions. Younger buyers are more likely to brag about a home automation system rather than a newly renovated kitchen. And, many plan to reconfigure the dining room as an office and workspace. For condos and apartment rentals, there is again a preference for smaller spaces that are flexible and multi-purpose. Industry surveys, often not that scientific, recommend that developers allocate space for informal get-togethers, gyms, bike storage, and dog parks. One of the more novel amenities is locating a dual dog wash/car wash business.

The process of home buying, once clustered toward the nuclear family, is undergoing significant change. The newest buyers are neither nuclear nor families. A 2013 inquiry by a California congressman has found an unusual dynamic among house buyers. Normally, about 85 percent of home sales are individuals purchasing with a mortgage. In 2013, only about 40 percent of home sales were like this. Forty percent were all cash, more than 15 percent were distressed sales, and five percent were flips.

A new type of homebuyer emerged during the recent housing recession. Giant institutional investors like Blackstone Corporation and Colony Capital began buying single-family homes and converting them into rental properties. It is estimated that they now own, en masse, two hundred thousand suburban homes. These "Ozzie and Harriet" type homes have become permanent rental properties that are professionally managed. Wall Street investors are betting that the rental stream from these homes can be packaged and sold like a corporate bond. It is too early to know whether this new investment model will succeed.

The rental model may resonate with a younger Digital Age generation that indicate they want to be flexible, mobile, and unburdened by housework. A real estate professor, Anthony Sanders, comments, "We've gone from a homeownership society to a renter's market. Unemployment, rapidly changing careers, and delayed marriages make it less likely that young people will buy a home." Adding to the unlikelihood of home ownership is a mountain of student debt.

It does not appear that the next generation of buyers value home ownership as we know it today. In an online magazine called *Atlantic Cities*, journalist Emily Badger observes, "Home ownership is...now a liability, not an ambition. It's an anachronism in an age when nothing remains permanent anymore, when no one stays in the same job—let alone the same city, or even the same career—long enough to dent a 30-year mortgage. Homeownership represents the opposite of all the values that economists say will matter from now on—flexibility, mobility, adaptability..."

This disruptive real estate paradigm is not suited for Boomers who wish to sell their suburban homes at a premium. Boomers can continue to age in place, but they will pay a price in isolation, distance, and escalating property taxes. Meanwhile, a younger generation will discover new activities to replace home maintenance and upkeep. Although the rental model may or may not succeed over the long run, it points to a generation that has different preferences. Even if they buy, they will be less committed to D.I.Y. projects, form smaller simpler households, and trade less "sweat equity" for home ownership.

Is It Simple?

We find illustration in a magazine that many Boomers are familiar with: *Real Simple*. The magazine began publishing in 2000, coinciding with the Internet expansion. It markets a clean, uncluttered life style, and a typical headline reads, "Six Clever Ways to Simplify Your Life." Today, the print version of the magazine, *Real Simple*, may face its own obsolescence—it sometimes offers free second subscriptions. A downsizing is taking place across the print world. Wood-paneled libraries are old school, and used bookstores are brimming over as Boomers clear their bookshelves. As the Internet economy moves forward, it will leave a wake of papyrus. Our stored memory is moving to the Internet. The idea of family scrapbooks and photo albums is quaint, along with the family rooms in which they are stored. Millennials move on; develop relationships with roommates, spouses, and babies (sometimes not in that order); and then post pictures of them all on Inger, Instagram, and other Internet photo-sharing sites. As Boomers confront the next stage of aging, they will realize that they cannot take it with them, and the younger generation does not want to take it at all.

Smartphones Reshape Everyday Habits and Habitats

While Baby Boomers may still be skeptical that the Internet has wrought so many changes, the confirmation can be found in their handbag or clipped to a belt loop. The smartphones we carry are a portable Internet. Over the past decade many activities have migrated to the phone in the form of apps and widgets. While Boomers may not use most of them, younger people do. Business processes are in flux, and Boomers will have to keep up with them, even if it means just hanging on to the coattails of new applications.

A pithy example of how habits change is an elder Boomer who tries to perform a familiar task: finding a phone number through the Yellow Pages or by dialing "O" for operator. Today, that is a trying process—the phone books are out of date as soon as they are printed and telephone operators are often clueless. Likewise, a Boomer who tries to book an airline ticket over the telephone will quickly realize that he or she needs a computer connection to sort through better deals. Soon, Boomers will realize that their boarding passes are sent to their smartphones, their medical records are stored online, and banking apps will replace the need to carry credit cards. Many day-to-day activities that used to be done in person, or by picking up a rotary phone, migrated first to the Internet, and were accessed on a desktop computer. Now these activities are moving onto an Internet-enabled smartphone, and possibly a smart-watch. The difference, and this is critical, is that instead of talking to another person at the other end of the phone line, or sitting in the privacy of their home, transactions on the smartphone are done in real time, anywhere, anytime, and without person-to-person assistance.

For Boomers who are more comfortable with email than social media, these changes may not seem so progressive. They may seem as strange as the self-check-out lines that are displacing baggers and clerks. However, Boomers are not inexperienced: they regularly use the automatic teller machines (ATMs) that were introduced in the 1980s and replaced many bank teller positions. The critical difference is that the ATM did not displace the need to travel to a banking outlet. Today, in an advanced Internet economy the banking can be completed online, replacing the need to travel.

Bytes for Bites

Banking is one thing, but it is hard to imagine that the smartphone will worm its way into our eating and leisure. But, in fact, an industry upheaval is taking place over our taste buds: Boomers like to smell the pizza and frequent the local dough maker while Digital Natives prefer to place orders for fast food over their smartphones and couple it with home delivery. As a consequence, the large pizza chains and franchises are gaining share while mom-and-pop pizza stores are in decline; the trend is attributed to digital ordering, as the big chains derive 40 percent or more of their orders from the Internet.

Although they may never enjoy placing their pizza order with a smartphone app, Boomers will adapt and learn new ways to engage with their family, friends, and businesses. But, their late adoption of Facebook provides some glimpse of the issue: Boomers may feel that they are giving up the quality of their discourse and their privacy. The modus operandi of the Boomer cohort has nurtured casual, and some would say, tenuous human interactions. The expression "Have a good day," exchanged between virtual strangers, encapsulates how little we know about each other but how we put ourselves, briefly and fleetingly, in a relationship of casual encounters.

The smartphone is the genesis for new ways to meet and greet. Most Boomers will remain in the dark about these—for them the smartphone is silent and soulless. They will be reluctant to bank by cell phone or find virtue in the "share economy." Importantly, they will not discover the *playful* side of the cell phone technology: most will not use the phone to spontaneously meet up with people, find rides, share short irreverent tweets, or complete online contests and games. And, Baby Boomers are unlikely to make new discoveries from the geographic capabilities of smartphones. To them, GPS navigation will be something they use in the car instead of paper maps. Boomers will question the privacy trade-offs of the smartphone.

Still, the small, handheld cell phone may bring supersized impacts to how we use our homes or apartments. Parents of teens already experience how phones compound their parental supervision, since kids have access to unfiltered information and pictures. Smartphones work like radar to pinpoint edgy trends.

Unlike an earlier generation that used a car to flee from their parents' homes, teens with smartphones are just fine if they walk or take public transportation. They can continue their texting and chatting throughout the trip. The cell phone is already impacting transportation trends, as teens are getting their driver's licenses later and driving less.

Things may be turning upside down for homeowners too. For the Boomers, home was where you rested, recreated, and entertained. For a younger generation, homes may be scaled- down, simpler places. There is little need for a big TV room and a suburban backyard when better recreational and social options take place outside the home. Crowd sourcing and mobile networking will displace traditional way of doing things. In the following table we preview some changes.

THE GAME CHANGER—BOOMERS AND TECHNOLOGY

Table 6: Getting Things Done, Smartphone vs. Cars

Activities & Errands	Hypothetical Millennial, age 20	Hypothetical Boomer, age 65
Shop for phone	Go online and sign new contract	Visit phone stores
Socialize with friends	Text, Snapchat	Phone and email, meet up
Learn a new language	Download app	Sign up for class at Extension
Movie night	Watch on iPad	Watch in family room on big TV
Work outside office	Use tablet or phone on –the- go	Work from home office
Go for drive	Access car share service or Uber/Lyft	Own Car (paid for)
Go for bike ride	Use hub bikes	Bike is in garage (first, fill tires)
Buy toothpaste, toilet paper	Amazon.com or the like	Drive to stores
Plan a vacation	Compile ideas online	Get guide book

191

Unlikely Companions

One of the paradoxes of new technology is that as people acquire more efficient means of transmitting information, they spend more time, *not less,* transmitting more information. The technology accelerates the amount and rate of information they consume. So, Digital Natives send more texts and do more searches online. Academics like Edward Glaeser speculate that younger people are congregating in urban settings, as cities magnify the diversity and speed of interaction. Meanwhile, there is less need to travel. Comparison shopping, say for a new appliance or camera lens, is easily done online. Trying out digital paint swatches may be preferable to visiting a paint store. Sprawl eats up time because of travel.

Another impact, which may explain why so many young people are preferring to live in urban areas, is that short commutes improve our face-to-face connections, while long commutes stretch our friendships, literally. The Internet and social media are reawakening an interest in the social interaction of a city.

Boomers, who are from the motor age, view smartphones as an unlikely companion. The Boomers are a generation that literally lined up at motor vehicle offices for their driving exam at age sixteen and have been pounding the road ever since. Boomers will never come to love their smartphones as much as cars, but they will be affected.

The Home Is Homely

This chapter began with a description of "disruptive technology." These are game changing inventions like the automobile and electricity. It would hardly seem that the smartphone, a physically small device, could have such supersized impacts. But, smartphones do change our established way of doing things. Digital Natives, who spend less time commuting, will find new activities to replace the weekday hours Boomers allocated for long daily commutes and the weekends spent driving for errands and activities. A younger generation, coming of age, seeks different diversions, and most of these are not in the home. Watching short video clips on the phone or tablet can take place anywhere, eating at restaurants reviewed on Chowhound is more exciting than cooking or food shopping, and bicycling is a better form of exercise and more fun than working out in the home gym. A designer, Marianne Cusato, describes it this way, "The closer you are to cafes and movie theaters, the smaller your house can be because it doesn't need to "do everything for you". This is a difficult concept to grasp, bit imagine a commuter who comes home from work, after navigating a busy freeway with angry drivers and nail-biting congestion. The last thing this commuter wishes to do is get back in the car and drive someplace anew. So, dinner is likely to be had at home, and the nice kitchen with granite countertops and shiny appliances is put to good use. On the other hand, a young Millennial, working from home throughout the day, might feel the need to go out and seek others. Put differently, if there is more to do nearby, the house carries less of an "entertainment burden." New homes may downsize, just as the homes of the Newport "400" eventually lost their ballrooms, bowling alleys, and libraries too.

This ethos carries a financial impact for Boomers. It whittles at the market value of suburban real estate. Like the hard-to-replace antiques we saw fall in value, these homes have less allure to younger buyers, particularly those with the best-paying, secure jobs. Boomers outfitted their properties with bells and whistles that suited the state of technology in the 1990s and 2000s. House sizes sprawled to accommodate a big kitchen–family room combo, the all-important media room, and home gyms. The bottom line is that these well-equipped homes are just that—places filled with "stuff." These homes are billowing, cavernous space when the stuff is no longer useful. Boomers will come to recognize that housing styles and trends are moving on, moving mobile.

Demographers who quantify these trends have noted that a "re-urbanization" is taking place. They do not foresee a net increase for suburban houses on larger lots. Instead, they predict new demand for attached units, like apartments, townhouses, and condos, and homes with very small lots. The next generation of Digital Natives is favoring more urban areas, but not necessarily downtown centers. They like neighborhoods, sometimes in mid-size cities or towns that can blend trendy shops, museums, sporting and concert venues, yoga, and an ethnic mix of restaurants and take-out. These desirable neighborhoods have two things in common: they provide opportunities to mingle and meet, and they are walkable. In larger cities, like San Francisco or Seattle, properties are more valuable if there is a bus or subway system nearby and a bicycle lane.

A spatial reorganization is taking place. When the Boomers came of age, they used cars to connect, and the age of sprawl spiraled out of proportion. Their willingness to drive pushed out traditional urban boundaries, and roads were redesigned around vast stretches of gas stations, fast food establishments, and chain stores. Boomers' fixation with cars also encouraged more novel developments that could blend driving, recreation, and business such as the factory outlet mall or the overnight vacation destination. Today, Digital Natives do their shopping online and prefer to bargain hunt in cyberspace instead of driving to the factory outlet store. As a consequence, suburban shopping centers are in decline; some have become empty storefronts with weed-filled parking lots. That was round one of the real estate shakeup. The second round, now gathering steam, will sweep through suburban homes as the Boomers retire. There is a crisis ahead—as Boomers are less able to drive, and Digital Natives are less inclined to.

CHAPTER EIGHT

CONCLUSIONS AND RECOMMENDATIONS

It's getting nighttime and Brenda and Elliot need to turn in. It is too dark to read, and Elliott puts down his Smart Phone. Brenda finishes her drink and casts a final glance over the expansive lawn, the pool and the RV. Brenda finally gets Eliot's attention and learns that he is quite happy to scuttle the vacation in the RV. In fact, he wonders why they didn't discuss this earlier! Lawn work...he says that's over too. Elliott says he is on board with a visit to the new townhouse project down the street, particularly if they have built-in high speed Internet.

We have explored forces that will continue to impact real estate values and the ability to age-in- place. The sheer number of Baby Boomers, born between 1946 and 1964, continues to be a tidal wave moving through the housing market. As young adults, Boomers confronted a shortage of suitable homes. Their demographic bulge ignited a building spree to far-flung suburban tracts. Contractors found it less expensive to develop land beyond urban perimeters, and Baby Boomers came to favor these suburban lots, with their bigger homes, expansive yards, and longer commutes. This is the generation that was first to invent many things, including a willingness to *drive till you qualify*.

The *drive till you qualify* was fueled, literally, by a surge in automobile ownership. The suburbs could not have grown without the car, and the car culture needed the suburbs to expand. Before the Baby Boomers, commuters lived closer to transit and households owned only one car, if any. Then the norm changed and the number of households owning two or more cars grew from 30 percent in 1969 to 77 percent by 2009. In 1990, as the car culture triumphed, one in six jobs in the United States was associated with the building, sales, repair, fueling, or parking of cars.

Today, the number of people employed in the car industry is shrinking while the number of employees working in computers and Internet businesses has expanded. Real estate values will be impacted as the motoring age fades, and the digital one progresses. Chapter Seven explored how the Internet is a disruptive technology for suburban homeowners. When commerce shifts online instead of in stores, the suburban landscape contracts. Local retailers shutter up and big businesses seek to relocate in central shopping areas so that they can attract regional shoppers. The strip-mall ends up with more vacancies, and the traffic to the mega-shopping center increases.

These changes come at a time when Boomers will have more leisure time to shop, but are less likely to drive. Younger people, who grew up in the suburbs, are showing little propensity to live there and are shunning a lifestyle built around driving to work and then driving to shop. Big companies are abandoning suburban campuses for urban offices so that they can recruit younger workers. And these younger workers are able to keep their employment options flexible when they relocate in urban areas that have more employment and educational opportunities nearby.

"Re-urbanization" seems like an alien concept to many Boomers. When they came of age, major U.S. cities, like Chicago and New York, were plagued with crime, poor schools, and, we might add, expensive and difficult parking. For a generation that worshipped the car, the difficult parking may have been an impediment on par with the crime and schools. But these cities have done a U-turn and improved their infrastructure. They have become desirable places to live. With the Internet, even the most intractable problems, like parking, seem to have solutions. Parking spaces are being freed up through time-of-use rates, and by car-share startups like Uber. Meanwhile, mid-sized cities and inner-ring suburbs have also grown in popularity. They offer amenities like public transportation, lively downtowns, and less car-dependent lifestyles. The children of the Baby Boomers are quick to use alternative transportation and slow to get driver's licenses. The decline of a car-centric culture has begun.

So, as we advance into an era in which smartphones connect everyone, what are the prospects for Baby Boomers who are adept with older technology? In the following sections, we provide some actionable items for Boomers, so that they stay aware of the trends and protect the quality of their retirement.

Action Item I: Take Stock of What Is Important

Some observers think that there will be a release of 26 million homes by 2030, and others have predicted 40 million surplus homes as Boomers retire. The scope is mind numbing. That does not mean that Baby Boomers should immediately rush to sell their homes. It does mean that Boomers should revisit their assumptions if they have planned to supplement their retirement income by using their homes as a "nest egg" or "ATM" machine.

Before the Baby Boom generation, home ownership was simpler. Homes, were *just* homes, and much less an investment. The Boomers' parents did not purchase properties with the expectation that they were buying an asset that would double or triple their wealth. That expectation began to change in the 1980s as home values accelerated.

When the music stopped, that is when house prices began to fall and the economy tanked in 2007, many homeowners held on—thinking that things would improve and they could recover their losses. Fortunately for the Baby Boomers, they had a lower foreclosure rate than younger generations.

The first action item is to accept that there are fundamental shifts in the real estate market, brought about by demographics and technological change. For Boomers this may mean decoupling themselves from the property they live in, both emotionally and financially. The emotional decoupling may be the hardest, since they have invested so much time and energy, as well as pride of ownership. But, if Boomers take stock of what is really important, is it going to be their large homes with upgraded appliances, or will it be the opportunity to go forward in good health with basic needs met?

When owning their home is separated from their quality of life Boomers can more objectively take stock of what comes next. They are less likely to tenaciously hold out for a real estate recovery. They are more likely to consider selling, investing the proceeds in a low risk security or bank account, and moving to a smaller property. When Boomers view their real estate, and particularly the stuff in it, as replaceable, they can comfortably make decisions that are best for them overall. They will be less likely to be led by market ups and down.

Action Item II: Review the Options - Study the Fine Print

There are large, reoccurring monthly fees if Boomers relocate to a retirement community now, or assisted living later. To even consider these changes, Boomers need to get their financial matters in order today by paying down their existing debt and in many cases, living leaner. Leaner living may involve difficult decisions like spinning off support for dependent children, downsizing to one car, or reducing the scope of vacation trips and travel. Financial advisor John Talbott put it this way, "part of the debt problem...is that families converted their 30 day credit card debt into 30 years mortgage debt through refinancing."

One option for living leaner is to make our homes produce income, while staying in residence. This works in geographic areas with a shortage of affordable housing and a high demand for rooms or guest quarters. Boomers who rent out rooms can offset their monthly expenses. They might also find it feasible to exchange rooms for assistance with transportation and errands. College towns and fast-growing urban areas are likely to be good places for these exchanges to take place.

The majority of Boomers are likely to think more conventionally and explore the equity they can draw out of their homes now. Potentially, they can pay off their mortgage debt and meet monthly expenses. In Chapter Five we explored the pluses and minuses of the reverse mortgage. We noted that average people have difficulty understanding the terms even with the personal financial counseling required by the government. If Boomers opt for a reverse mortgage, they need impartial eyes to go over the contract. Will the promise of monthly income be a fair exchange for the back-end costs? What are the underlying actuarial assumptions of how long they will continue to live there? Are these realistic?

Before signing, the most vital question is whether there is sufficient cash to maintain the home. To avoid foreclosure, the homeowner must be on time with state and federal taxes, insurance, certain home repairs, and/or homeowner's fees. It would be prudent to build an inflation factor into these expenses, and realize that the reverse mortgage may seem like a bad deal in a time of high inflation.

With reverse mortgages also comes the thorny issue of inheritance. Boomers should evaluate what, if anything, they will pass down to heirs. It takes planning so that the mortgage title is recorded properly and that a surviving spouse or partner is not evicted. Still, the best lawyer cannot keep the property in the family estate if the mortgage exceeds the home's appraised value and there is no other equity to pay it off. In many cases the reverse mortgage will spell the end of a property inheritance.

Reverse mortgage lenders are primed to grow because these mortgages are the "ATM machine" of last resort. Many Boomers are using the reverse mortgage before they fully retire to pay down their debts. This may exhaust the windfall. For those who can wait, the reverse mortgage may seem like the remedy to cover assisted living fees or in-house caretakers. This is a likely scenario if end-of-life costs overwhelm the budget. Staying healthy and maintaining coverage for long-term care are new twists on keeping the household financially intact. Otherwise, "banking on the house" with a reverse mortgage will be the final option.

Action Item IIa— A Subset for Women

This action item is a subset of items I and II, which takes stock of housing needs and income streams as people age. Younger Boomers routinely overlook the significance of gender. The demographic facts are that older women simply outnumber older men. Women have a longer life expectancy, combined with the propensity to marry older spouses.

This has practical implications for housing. As people age in place after their children move out, these houses have too many bedrooms and too few occupants. This is compounded when a spouse dies. This should give pause to older women, since they will be living in and maintaining these large houses. In 1995, well before the current bulge of Baby Boom retirements, 9.8 million persons age 65 or older lived alone. Eight in ten (77 percent) of these were women. Not only will more older women live alone in these big homes— they are also more likely to be unassisted and isolated. Women stop driving sooner than men, drive shorter distances, and have less overall mobility in their old age than men. They may be the first group to experience suburbs that incarcerate them.

Boomers who have taken care of elderly parents can testify to the distress when older people, usually widowed, stay in their homes, but have little outside support. Some complain that the bills are not paid on time, while others speak of the home repairs that go undone, and the safety hazards that mount with reduced eyesight or trying to drive. It is an irony that Boomer women, who have worked so hard to afford these family homes, could find them to be an albatross as they age. Action Item V has the most practical advise but there is no single solution.

Action Item III: An Alternative Transportation Plan

As Boomers plan for retirement they must evaluate the options when their driving trips are cut back or become off limits. Would reduced mobility impact their qualify of life or could they adapt? Past generations, like their parents, did not experience this problem because their life expectancies were shorter, they had fewer cars, and they did not live in remote suburbs.

One of the constants as people age is that they drive less, not only because it becomes more difficult and less safe for them, but also because they risk the lives of others too. Accidents maim and kill passengers, pedestrians, and other drivers. That is probably the reason that older people generally self-regulate their driving and voluntarily cut back as they age. Whether Baby Boomers will do so is unknown, since they have had a lifelong affinity and dependence on cars.

The ability to walk to shops and other places is a vital consideration if Boomers turn in their car keys. Interestingly, locating near doctors' offices may be valuable too. It turns out that trips for medical visits are the fastest growing trip type among Boomers. Suburbs that are reached by public transportation may provide the best option for able-bodied Boomers, and transit usually passes by the larger medical centers. But, as people age they find it more difficult to use public transportation because they have to do things like board and exit quickly, and climb up steps to the vehicle or to the station. Public transportation will not fit all situations.

New mobility options (cited in Chapter Three) are beginning to appear. One promising development is the Car Club, and we will have more to say about this in our last action item. Boomers who want to maintain an element of personal control and independence need to think forward, to picture how they would continue to live in their homes if the garage and the car were off-limits. Would they be solitary and alone or could they do the most basic things, like get groceries and go to the doctor? Some Boomers will reason that their homes are not in desirable locations, but they will be able to depend on friends and family to help them with these basics. That is a solution, providing that these friends and family stay in geographic proximity.

Given the amorous relationship that Boomers have with their cars, it is doubtful that they will want to spend their senior years being escorted in ten-passenger Dial-A-Ride vans or scaled-down, senior friendly, school buses. For many, mobility may be of higher importance than aging in place. In that case, it may be best to deal with this insecurity now and consider renting or owning elsewhere. Many older suburbs like Brookline, Massachusetts, and Silver Spring, Maryland, have public transportation. Smaller towns like Asheville, North Carolina and Bend, Oregon, are walkable. According to *U.S. News* the ten (best) places to go carless in retirement are: Amherst, Massachusetts; Ann Arbor, Michigan; Berkeley, California; Boone, North Carolina; Boulder, Colorado; Corvallis, Oregon; Ithaca, New York.; Princeton, New Jersey; Pullman, Washington; and State College, Pennsylvania. It is noteworthy that big cities with transit, like Chicago or San Francisco, are not listed. Transit is not a sufficient criteria; the areas must also be accessible and affordable.

Although Boomers can move to areas with public transportation, they may find using transit is slow and cumbersome, having spent a lifetime behind the steering wheel. The shared autonomous vehicle (SAV) may be the brightest spot on the transportation horizon for Boomers. It may be too early to relocate to areas where the driverless (SAV) vehicles will be prototyped but it is not too early for seniors to lobby their representatives and insurance companies to speed up the inevitable legal wrangles and infrastructure development. If Boomers have a single opportunity to change the world in their retirement, it is in quickly adapting to this new mobility. The SAV may be able to transverse the vast, spread distances of the suburbs in a way that has never been economical or practical for public transportation.

Action Item IV:

Involved with Technology

Here we switch gears. Although no one truly understands what we will do with the nanny robots and few people know how two-way cameras will change aging in place, it is a good idea to take stock of these changes. We have seen, throughout this book, that the Internet is a driver of change, literally, in the case of future SAV vehicles. Most Boomers will be using smartphones, perhaps flipping between a call to their children and summoning their home-friendly robot.

It is essential, going forward, that Boomers accept that change is the new norm, and then do their homework to stay abreast of it. In Chapter Seven we observed how tasks that have moved to the Internet make it frustrating to now look up an address on paper or book a reservation over the telephone. Boomers did not grow up using the Internet and smartphones, but they must learn new skills if they are going to remain useful members of society. The Boomer who exclusively checks his or her giant TV screen for news and information will lag behind and not understand cultural trends. To keep pace with a younger generation, and keep open lines of communication with them, Boomers will need to be more tech-savvy.

The good thing about keeping pace with new technologies is that they may have a bonus for health and well-being. There is a burgeoning industry creating mind games, puzzles, and brain exercises for seniors. Learning how to download an application from the

Internet, or programming a smartphone for navigation are real-life exercises for the brain as well as survival tools.

There will be a surge in computer classes, like the ones currently held at Apple Stores and public libraries. It is stimulating to imagine Boomers, now retired, exchanging electronic files of their favorite '60s and '70s rock bands and posting their own sound recordings. Perhaps a favored recording will actually be the Beatles song, "Baby You Can Drive My Car!"

In order to tune into the society, Boomers must tune into the technology that is "driving it." They can do most of this in their homes, if they so choose. While mastering the technology may spell many hours of frustration, it may lead to curiosity, and later, to entertainment or education. Boomers need to be conversant with newer technology, unless they decide to be irreverent, outdated, and cast aside.

Action Item V: Age with Community

This last item brings us full circle. Boomers will recall that one of the most-read books in the late 1960s was called *The Whole Earth Catalog*. The catalog was the brainchild of Stewart Brand in San Francisco, and he provided inspiration and illustrations for things like building your own yurt, using solar power, and reducing waste. After 1972 it was published only sporadically.

The essence of *The Whole Earth Catalog* was creating tools that could be shared among the youthful counter-culture. Brand began with grassroots ideals and the startling covers of deep space and the planets promoted an Earth Day awareness. It is not surprising that by the 1970s Brand decided that his early stance of emphasizing individualism should be replaced with one favoring community.

It is arguable whether a more harmonious, less cruel society has been created in the thirty-five years since the last big catalog. The Boomers who first thumbed through *The Whole Earth Catalog* in their dorm rooms and small apartments then moved on to their far-flung suburban homes. But, in some ways, the objectives of the whole earth movement were never left behind. When the real estate market collapsed in 2007, Boomers were left with a fragile reawakening to core values that did not begin and end with a dollar sign.

Coming full circle we have seen two or three examples where a "whole earth" approach brings dividends for Boomers. Most distinctly in Chapter Seven, we discussed material possessions and how a trend to "lighten up" liberates people to do other things. Although Boomers have spent a lifetime accumulating the likes of better headphones, appliances, built-ins, and TVs there is a chilling knowledge that they cannot take these things with them, and that they are not so essential. As financial advisor John Talbott put it, "people run back into their burning homes to save their children and pets and pictures, but no one risks their life to save a sofa, television, or washing machine."

The community values professed in *The Whole Earth Catalog* are vital ones for Boomers to learn as they resolve aging-in-place issues. Transportation is a key concern. With the Internet as background, and the share economy as foreground, older people have acquired options to share cars and rides. The share economy is likely to reinvent personal transportation and make it more feasible for Boomers to age in place, if that is their true wish. The next cusp of change is housing itself. The share economy may help Boomers identify renters for their guest quarters, downsize possessions, and discover fellow Boomers with similar needs.

The village model, which was cited in Chapter Five, started in 2001 as the Internet was growing, and it will continue to transform with it. Only fifteen years ago, there was a single group called the Beacon Hill Village in Boston with a mission to help seniors remain in their homes and age with peace of mind. The model is so useful that today there are more than eighty village communities in the United States alone. Some of the services they provide are rides, help with pets, assistance with paperwork, and member-hosted events. But, they are far more comprehensive than a driving exchange or a means to locate a vetted handyman. Their concierge-like services require person-to-person neighborliness supported by computers, smartphones, and databases. The village model will only expand as Boomers stay-put and the technology makes it more feasible to assist them in far-flung suburbs.

ACKNOWLEDGEMENTS

When my grandfather, Isaac, got too old to drive he parked his beloved Studebaker Torpedo near Yankee Stadium, turned over the keys to a friend, and walked back home to the apartment he shared with my grandmother. Fast forward. When both my father and mother, Jerry and Jen, got too old to drive they continued to anyway, because they lived in a newer suburban home at the end of a long cul-de-sac, situated by a state-highway. There was no alternative.

This book grew out of that reflection. It came to fruition however, from a class taught at UCLA by Professor Marty Wachs in Spring 2012 on aging and transportation. I was happy to be invited as an end-of-term guest. Others who have inspired my career in transportation include Tom Golob, Elaine Murakami, Sandra Rosenbloom, and the MST program at MIT. I would like to thank them all and also acknowledge some writer friends including Linda Tampkin, Sam

Barry at Book Passage, and Mandy Ericson, a capable editor.

Getting the book on paper would not have been possible without my three sons, John, Ted, and William. John made it clear from the beginning that social media was a link to better publishing. Ted was the go-to source for legal issues and San Francisco tech. William was at-my side checking references, updating charts, and downloading new software.

My biggest thank you and infinite gratitude goes to my husband, Walter. He never doubted that this would get into print, and provided many hours of learned counsel and advice on real-estate markets and finance. I appreciate the help of so many friends and family who made this book possible. Of course, all errors and omissions remain the responsibility of the author.

INDEX

AARP, 23, 75, 110, 114,
138
Age in place
car dependency, 19, 44,
52, 90
kid dependency, 150–
53
planning steps, 17
polls about, 16
tap home equity, 110

Badger, Emily, 183
Beacon Hill Village, 85,
134
Blackstone, 182
Blockbuster, 163
Boomburb, 58
Boomers
debt, 24, 48, 54, 55,
109–10, 111, 118,
206
energy use, 103
inheritance, next gen,

11, 115–16, 151–53
location of homes, 39,
70
love for cars, 67–72,
200
love for kids, 140
new technology, 189,
215
number retiring, 30
reinvention of things,
84
sprawl, 57
Brand, Stewart, 217

Cars. *See also* Driverless
car
alternative schemes,
85
car dependency, 58,
210
car share worldwide,
178
chauffeurs, 23, 90, 149

cutting back, 69, 78
digital alternatives, 191
driving safety, 18, 77,
    154
expansive growth,
    Boomers, 68–72
Case-Shiller index, 55
Center for Neighborhood
    Technology, 92
Children, 139–55, *See*
    also Millennials,
    Digital Natives
Colony Capital, 182
Cusato, Marianne, 194

Delivery to home, 188,
    See Retail
    7-11 ideas, 101
    health care, 20, 83
Demographics, 34–37
    "demographic
        crossroads", 123
    science of population,
        29
Detroit, 28, 44, 51
Digital Natives, 166–73,
    197
    sea change, 122
Disruptive technology,
    158, 168
drive till you qualify, 6,
    51, 57, 70, 73, 78, 91,
    93, 105, 158, 200
Driverless car, 9, 85, 89,
    96, 106, 214

Edge city, 58
Energy pig, 26, 97
Environment, 95–102,
    125
Exurbs, 57

Families
    divorce, 145
    modern demographics,
        29, 42, 64, 121
    suburban poor, 155
Funding retirement, 111
    home as piggybank,
        49, 120
    shortfalls, 23, 43

Gallagher, Leigh, 123
Gallup, 148
Garage, 40, 58, 64
Glaeser, Edward, 192
Goodwill stores, 180

Hartog Hendrik, 151
Health
    and driving, 9, 70, 76
    and exercise, 22
    and learning, 215
Home Depot, 56
Houses
    dated, old features, 61,
        65, 97–99, 104, 159,
        166, 194
    home ownership rates,
        36, 37
    rental trend, 123, 182

rethink of value, 3, 24, 123, 183
spatial mismatch, 40, 64
the cost of moving on, 129–38
transportation costs, 91–93
upkeep of older, 21
Housing meltdown
and reverse mortgage, 117
cash trend, 181
in the future, 203
past, 2007-2011, 3, 122
HUD, 114

Immigration, 29, 41, 44, 64, 122
Interest rates, 49
Internet, 71, 73, 87–89, 166–97
reshape everyday habits, 185–93
The death of "things" material, 173–85
The death of distance, 168–72

Kiplinger, 119
Kotkin, Joel, 154
Kotlikoff and Burns, 111
Kunstler, James Howard, 73

Lyft, 26, 88, 191

Millennials, 27, 124
debt, 147, 182
delayed licenses, 91, 190
missing households, 150
preferences for homes, 91, 102, 145, 181, 196
preferences for mobility, 96, 121
when marry, 154
Mortgages, 108, *See* Reverse mortgage
and policy, 50
and turned down, 112
income tax deduction, 125
Multifamily homes, 56
Multigenerational household, 147, 151

National Association of Home Builders, 98
National Institute on Aging, 18
National System of Interstate, 52
Nelson, Arthur, 99
Newport, RI, 160, 175
NORC. *See* Retirement, relocation

Ozzie and Harriet, 38, 102, 140, 182

Paratransit. *See* Public transportation
Parker, Kim, 147
Pew Foundation, 147, 150
Public transportation, 19, 60, 74, 80–81, 126, 196, 213
    access to, 17
    Millennials and, 121
    vs. building roads, 52

Real Simple, 184
Retail, 59
    before the Internet, 56
    with the Internet, 177–80, 201
Retirement. *See* Houses; The Cost of Moving on; Funding Retirement
    relocation, 129–38, 212–13
Reverse mortgage, 112–19, 206–8
    as investment strategy, 118
    balloon like, 116
    lenders, 114
    pitfalls, 114
Roads, 87, *See* National System of Interstate
Robots, 20, 83, 167, 215
Rock 'n Roll, 15, 216

Rosenbloom, Sandy, 81

Sanders, Anthony, 182
SAV. *See* Driverless car
Share economy, 174–73, 219
Silent Generation, 108, 110, 113, 117
Smartphone, 71, 87–89, 185–93
Social interaction
    in suburbia, 38
    in urban areas, 193
    nanny robots, 21
    smartphone, 187
Sprawl, 59, 73, 126, 192, 197, *See* Boomers
SB375, 105, 126
    vs. urban homes, 164
Streetcar, 57, 59

Talbott, John, 109, 206, 218
Taxi, 88
The National Association of Realtors, 123
The Whole Earth Catalog, 217
Time use, 51, 102, 183, *See* also Millennials
Transportation, 67, *See* cars, driverless cars, public transportation, streetcars

Uber, 26, 88, 89, 191, 202

Villages, 134, 219

Walking, 58, 75, 76, 196,

213
Wealth effect, 54
Women, older, 21, 37, 79, 124, 209–10
Woodstock, 15

REFERENCES

INTRODUCTION

1. More than 50% of the U.S. population have been in their current homes 10 to 19 years: Paul Emrath, "How Long Buyers Remain in Their Homes," Special Studies, February, 2009. National Association of Home Builders. The data is from the 2007 American Community Survey (ACS).

2. The Boomers, and older age groups, own nearly 60 percent: see Table I in Chapter One. Note: the data is only for owner-occupied homes. In 2008, the source year for some of the data, the youngest boomers were only forty-four years old and the oldest were sixty-two.

3. 21 percent of the population over age 65 do not drive. This is an average, based on 27% non-drivers among women and 11% non-drivers among men. The authors note there are still more female drivers age 65+ on the road than males because of their greater numbers. Jana Lynott and Carolos Figueiredo, "How the Travel Patterns of Older Adults are Changing: Highlights from the 2009 National Household Travel Survey. AARP Public Policy Institute.

CHAPTER ONE: GROWING UP WITH THE CAR

4. Candlestick Park and "Baby You Can Drive my Car":
this song is the opening track for British release in 1965 of
"Rubber Soul" and the North America "Yesterday and Today"
collection (source: Wikipedia). Just recently, the song was again
a newsworthy headline: *"Candlestick farewell makes up for
Beatles failing in '66-but baby, you couldn't drive your car"*.
There was such a large traffic jam at Candlestick Park (San
Francisco) to see McCartney that thousands of concertgoers had
to listen from an idling car outside the stadium. *San Francisco
Chronicle*, August 16, 2014, Datebook.

5. when polled, three out of four Americans: Teresa
Keenan, "Home and Community P references of the 45+
Population," AARP Research, November, 2012. This is based on
a survey of 1,616 adults, ages 45 and older, conducted in 2010.
The AARP has asked this item in periodic surveys, and the
responses results are stable over time.

6. Are you in love with your home: *Kiplinger Retirement
Report*, July, 2014. page 6. The full page ad is for the "Easy
Climber," an elevator like device for multi-storied homes. The
text promotes stay-at-home values, *"The key to the American
Dream is to maintain independence and to live safely and
securely..."*

**7. Only 17 percent of Baby Boomers of Boomers live in
dense urban cities:** Jae Seung Lee, Christopher Zegras, Eran
Ben-Joseph, and Sungjin Park, "Does Urban Living Influence
Baby Boomers' Travel Behavior?" *Journal of Transport
Geography*, No. 35, February 2014. The data is from the
Department of Transportation NHTS for 2005 and 2011.

8. Researchers at the National Institute on Aging published a paper in 2002 that estimated people will outlive: Daniel Foley, Harley Heimovitz, Jack Furalnik, and Dwight Brock, "Driving Life Expectancy of Persons Aged 70 Years and Older in the United State, *American Journal of Public Health*, August, 2002. The authors suggest that on average, male drivers age 70 to 74 will be dependent on alternative sources of transportation for approximately 7 years and that female drivers of the same age will be dependent on alternative sources of transportation for approximately 10 years. Debra Whitman, AARP Executive Vice President for Policy, also cited these numbers more recently. See, Ann Brenoff, "Elderly Driving: AARP Study Look at What Happens When Boomers Hang Up Their Car Keys," *The Huffington Post*, Nov. 9, 2012.

9. An estimated 70 percent of Baby Boomers: The 70% is based on an estimate from the J.S. Lee paper, *op. cit.* In the same paper, the locations that are denser and in closer proximity to urban areas (so-called 'second cities') have a transit share of only 1.4%, a bike share of 1.1% and 9.8% for bikes. A paper by M. Sarkar of the U.S. Census Bureau studied neighborhood characteristics. It estimates that 32.5% of owner occupied homes have public transportation. The estimate is not broken-out by age group. Mousumi Sarkar, "How American Homes Vary by the Year they were Built," Working Paper No. 2011-18. U.S. Census Bureau.

10. This industry forecasts growth: Sally Abrams, "New Technology Could Allow You or Your Parents to Age at Home," AARP Bulletin. March 2014. She is citing Laurie Orlov, an aging-in-place technology expert.

11. it is exercise, not puzzles, that maintain the aging brain: Beth Levine, "Exercise, Not Pu zzles, May Protect Aging Brain," AARP Bulletin. Jan. 7, 2013. Researchers at the University of Edinburgh studying nearly 700 people in their early 70s, found that those who were most physically active had less brain shrinkage than those who got less exercise.

12. home equity represented 80 percent: Ashlea Ebeling, "A Troubling Housing Misstep by Boomers, " *Forbes*, March 19, 2012. This quote is from Stephanie Moulton, commenting on the 2007 Survey of Consumer Finance.

13. The AARP reports that thirty-four percent of Americans: Amy Traub and Demos, "In The Red: Older Americans and Credit Card Debt," Middle Class Security Project. AARP Public Policy Institute. January, 2013.

14. One of the most startling trends is the number of people carrying mortgage debt as they age: Lori Trawinki, "Nightmare on Main Street: Older Americans and the Mortgage Market Crisis," AARP Public Policy Institute, 2012.

15. Only 54 percent of the adult population is married and single person households rose to 27% in 2010: Jonathan Vespa, Jamie M. Lewis, and Rose M. Kreider, "America's Families and Living Arrangements: 2012 Population Characteristics," U.S. Census Bureau. August 2013.

16. "energy hogs": The pig, as analogy, might have begun with a 2005-06 Ad Council Campaign for energy efficiency. See http:/en.wikipedia.org/wiki/Energy_Hog.

17. (young professionals) choose to: Ellen Huet, "How Tech Became the Enemy- Then and Now," *San Francisco Gate*, March 24, 2014.

18. 6,000 people a day reach age 65: http://www.statisticbrain.com/retirement-statistics.

19. Dateline (Florida-2003: Fred Brock, "Seniority; A Soft Landing for Boomers" *The New York Times*, July 13, 2003.

20. Dateline (blog, 2010):"Normaward," Blogspot, "A Troubling Housing Misstep by Boomers," Forbes, March 19, 2012.

21. Dateline: Ferguson, MO (2013): The statistic about Ugly Homes was reported in *The Boston Globe*. The testimonial is from the company web site. www.homevestors.com /testimonials/ accessed August 4, 2014.

22. Dateline: Wall Street (2013): Tara Bernard, "Rules for Reverse Mortgages May Become mo re Restrictive," *The New York Times*, July 12, 2013.

23. The Census Charts: "Aging in the United States- Past, Present, and Future," a report done in conjunction with the National Institute on Aging. http://www.census.gov/population/international/files/97agewc /pdf

24. a renowned economics paper that predicted: N. Gregory Mankiw and David Weil, "The Baby Boom, The Baby Bust and the Housing Market," *Regional Science and Urban Economics*, 1, 1989.

25. One conservative estimate predicts that: Judy Martel, "Boomers to swamp housing market?" *BankRate*, May 7, 2012. The number comes from a Bipartisan Policy Center report. A more extreme view is that there will be a surplus of 40 million homes. Professor Arthur Nelson, a demographer at the University of Utah, provides insight into the myriad of factors. See Arthur Nelson, **Reshaping Metropolitan America**, Island Press. 2013. For another overview read: John Pitkin and Dowell Myers, "U.S. Housing Trends, Generational Changes and the Outlook to 2050," Transportation Research Board and the Division on Engineering and Physical Sciences. Special Report 298. 2008.

26. Who Owns Homes (Table 1): Based on Sandra Colby and Jennifer Ortman, "The Baby Boom Cohort in the United States: 2012 to 2060. Current Population Reports," P25-1141. U.S. Census Bureau. Washington, D.C. May, 2014. Part two is an analysis by Dr. Sheharyari Bokhari, commissioned by the author, of the 2008-2012 American Community Survey Public Use Micro Data. The data is for Owner Occupied Household Units, n=75,239,229, not for all properties. Note that the sixty percent includes the Boomers, and older cohorts.

27. Baby Boom Population by Region (Table 2): "Selected Characteristics of Baby Boomers 42 to 60 Years Old in 2006," Age and Special Populations Branch. U.S. Census Bureau. Population Division.

28. it is said that the average 1950s home (in Canada): mjperry. blogspot.com/2011/08/another-chart-of-day-average-home-size.html.

29 . if a net immigration of 1.2 million people per year continues: Natalia Siniavskaia, "Immigrants and Housing Demand, National Association of Home Builders," Special Reports, August 3, 2012. The results for 2020 are based on a large simulation model, using current immigration trends. See also, John Pitkin and Dowell Myers, "U.S. Housing Trends: Generational Changes and the Outlook to 2050, " Special Committee Report 298. Transportation Report Board, 2008

30. Big Homes and Small Families (Table 3): Jonathan Vespa, Jamie M. Lewis, and Rose M. Kreider, "America's Families and Living Arrangements: 2012 Population Characteristics," U.S. Census Bureau, August 2013. Also, Rose Kreider and Diana Elliott. "Historical Changes in Stay-at-home-Mothers: 1969-2009," paper presented to the American Sociological Association. 2010 Annual Meeting. Atlanta, Ga. The average household size (for 3 time periods) is from statista, a statistics portal. www.statista.com/statistics/183648/average-size-of-households-in-the-us/. Finally, the source for median and

average square feet is:
www.census.gov/const/C25Ann/sftotalmedavgsqft.pdf

31. However, recent polls of seniors ages 60-plus: See, for example, studies by the Center for Retirement Research at Boston College. We are citing a September 23, 2013 presentation by Annamaria Lusardi and Olivia Mitchell.

32. The Boomer's average home price dropped by approximately... Patrick Simmons, "Are Aging Baby Boomers Abandoning the Single-Family Nest?" Fannie Mae Housing Insights, Vol. 4, Issue 3, June 12, 2014.

33. Housing stock is durable, while the population and its tastes change: Emily Badger, "America's Housing Stock Mismatch," *The Atlantic Cities*, September 27, 2011.

Chapter Two: Drive Till You Qualify

33. The median net worth of Baby Boomers was 8 percent lower: Carol Hymowitz, "Baby Boomers: Poorer in Old Age Than Their Parents," *Bloomberg Businessweek*, January 3, 2014. The article observes that the Boomers have a critical problem. In the aftermath of the recession many lost their jobs at a critical point in their productive years.

34. The Social Security administration projects that only 40% of Boomers:
www.ssa.gov/policy/docs/ssb/v65n3/v65n3p1. They estimate that only about 40 percent of the Boomers will meet be able to retire with a high level of financial security. Another 40 percent will replace less than three-quarters of their preretirement earnings. And, 20 percent will replace less than half of their preretirement earnings. The conventional planning advice

recommends post retirement income savings that replace 70 to 80 percent of pre-retirement income.

35. Part of the loss has occurred because of pensions:
Hymowitz, *op. cit.* For more research on the state of retirement savings see studies by the AARP Public Policy Institute and the Center for Retirement Research at Boston College. One important factor was a switch in the 1980's from pension plans to 401(k) accounts. These accounts were decimated by the recession but are recovering; also, many Boomers did not fund their 401(k) accounts until they were in their 40s.

36. Average 30 year Fixed interest rates by decade (chart data): www.freddiemac.com/pmms/pmms30.htm. The high is 18.45% in October, 1981.

37. The GI bill regulated government-insured mortgages: Patrick Doherty and Christopher Leinberger, "The Next Real Estate Boom," *op. cit.*

38. Drive till you qualify: This term was coined in the 1980s. For a modern perspective on it see Michael Lewyn at www.planetizen.com/node/66698. He says the connection between suburbia and cheaper housing is not a law of nature and that cheap suburban development was underwritten by public subsidies.

39. A number of Boomers did not actually become home owners until the 1990s: David Berson and Eileen Neely, "Homeownership in the United States: where we've been: where we're going." *Business Economics*, July 1997.

40. It also helped stimulate large home purchases, vacation properties: For an analysis of consumer spending patterns before/after the 2007 recession, see Alan Blinder, *After the Music Stopped*, Penguin Books, 2013.

41. Federal policy was revamped to extend home ownership: Luci Ellis, "Eight Policy Lessons from the US Housing Meltdown." *Housing Studies*, Vol. 26. Oct-Nov. 2011.

42. The scope of wealth effects is a topic of longstanding interest: John Gist, Carlos Figueiredo, and Satyendra Verma, "Housing Wealth Effects, Boomer Refinancing, Housing Debt, and Retirement Saving Adequacy- 1989-2007." Society of Actuaries, 2009. See also Matteo Iacovello, "Housing Wealth and Consumption," Board of Governors, Federal Reserve System, International Finance Discussion Papers. Number 1027, August, 2011.

43. homes appreciated by as much as 72 percent according to one index and just 34 percent: Alan Blinder, *op. cit.* Case-Shiller results are compared with an index maintained by the FHFA. Blinder says that the essential difference is that the government index does not include jumbo mortgages and subprime ones. However, the Case-Shiller index may overstate the percentage, because it is weighed towards more volatile urban areas on the East and West Coast.

44. credit card balances for the cohort aged 55 to 64 grew from $2,900 in 1989 to $6,900 in 2007: Elizabeth Nolan Brown, "Boomers Spending Less on Leisure, More on Education, Mortgage Interest, Adult Kids," AARP. September 13, 2012. The author is citing original research by Pamela Villarreal for the National Center for Policy Analysis.

45. The average Home Depot Store: htpps://corporate.homedepot.com/ourcompany/history/pages/default.aspx Also, en.wikipedia.org/wiki/The_Home_Depot.

46. Neologism: A neologism is a new word or a phrase that may be in the process of entering common use. According to Wikipedia, *Edge City* was popularized in 1991 by Joel Garreau, a Washington Post reporter. The first citation of *Boomburb* seems to be in a 2001 paper by Robert Lang and Patrick Simmons for the Fannie Mae Foundation.

47. Metropolitan areas covered almost twice as much land as they did at the start: Lopez, Russell (2014) "Urban Sprawl in the United States: 1970-2010," Cities and the Environment (CATE): Vol. 7: Issue 1, Article 7.

48. The high-density walking city of 1900 has been replaced: Chenghuan Chu, Edward Glaeser, and Matthew Kahn. "Job Sprawl: Employment Location in U.S. Metropolitan Areas," The Brookings Institution. Metropolitan Policy Program. July 2001.

49. Census and household data: "U.S. Census Bureau Reports Men and Women Wait Longer to Marry," U.S. Census Newsroom. Nov. 10, 2010. See also, Jonathan Vespa, Jamie M. Lewis, and Rose M. Kreider. "America's Families and Living Arrangements: 2012 Population Characteristics." U.S. Census Bureau. August 2013.

Chapter Three: Transportation- "The Key" Problem for Boomers

50. Over the past four decades car ownership nearly tripled.... National Household Travel Survey (NHTS) data is summarized by Nancy McGuckin and Jana Lynott. The study is called "Impact of Baby Boomers on US Travel, 1969 to 2009," AARP Public Policy Institute. This is also the source of the statistic that Boomers drive 17% more miles than other groups (as of 2009).

51. In 1980 the one-way average commute time..."Commuting in the United States- 2009," American

Community Survey Reports, U.S. Census Bureau. September, 2011. See also www.census.gov/hhes/commuting/

52. An unexpected outcome of these working families was even more driving...McGuckin and Lynott, *op. cit.* They say that the shift from traditional household-based tasks to "outsourced" good and services that required travel contributed the a fivefold increase in what planners call "maintenance trips."

53. It is estimated that for each vehicle we own: persquaremile.com/2011/01/20/800-million-spaces-and-nowhere-to-park/

54. While the number of parking spaces grew, jobs did not: Transportation Energy Data Book, Oak Ridge National Laboratory, Table 10.17.

55. There is also industry-wide recognition that the Boomer cohort: Michelle Maynard, "The Secret Fear of the Worlds Biggest Auto Companies," *Forbes*, January 21, 2013. A GFK automotive story shows that Gen X and Gen Y will account for more car sales than the Baby Boomers. However, a *BusinessWeek* story refutes this: http://www.businessweek.com/articles/2013-08-29/in-car-buying-baby-boomers-surpass-the-young.

56. James Howard Kunstler, *The Geography of Nowhere*, Touchstone. New York, 1993.

57. The AARP projects that by 2025 one in every five drivers...Jana Lynott and Carlos Figueiredo, "How The Travel Patterns of Older Adults are Changing: Highlights from the 2009 National Household Transportation Survey," AARP Public Policy Institute, April 2011.

58. Specialists use the term "transportation disability" when a medical condition: Ann Dellinger, "Describing the

Older Adult Population," in *Aging America and Transportation: Personal Choices and Public Policy*, eds. J. Coughlin and L. D'Ambrosia, 2012. Dellinger cites a 2001 analysis of the National Household Travel Study. They estimate that 23% of older adults, or 7.5 million people, have a transportation disability. The analysis was done for the FHWA (FWHA-PL-05-015) by Liss, McGuckin, Moore and Reuscher.

59. teens are involved in more accidents: Leonard Evans, "Reducing Older Road-User Deaths" in Coughlin and D'Ambrosio, *op. cit.* Evans compares the risks for three family members, a twenty-year old son, a forty-five year old dad, and a seventy-year old granddad. The twenty-year old son is the most likely to die as a driver, to be in a crash, and to kill another driver on the road (p. 146).

60. By 2020 eight states will have 20 percent of their population age 65 or older: Ann Dellinger, "Describing the Older Population" in Coughlin and D'Ambosio, *op. cit.*

61. A recent National Household Travel Survey found: Jana Lynott and Carolos Figueiredo, *op.cit.*

62. Both men and women are likely to live beyond the time that they can drive safely, as much as 6 years for men and about 10 for women: Daniel J. Foley, et al, *op. cit.*

63. putting faith in paratransit is just perpetrating: Sandra Rosenbloom, "Roadblocks Ahead for Seniors Who Don't Drive," Working paper, Innovation in Infrastructure, The Urban Institute, May 2013.

64. the largest growth of trip making among Boomers has been for medical services: Nancy McGuckin and Jana Lynott, *op. cit.*

65. The delivery of medical services: The 2012 data is from the U.S. Bureau of Labor Statistics, Occupational Outlook Handbook. http://www.bls.gov/ooh/healthcare/home-health-aides.htm.

66. Carbnb: City CarShare press release. http://citycarshare.org/june-17-2014-city-carshare-partners-next-village-san-francisco-expand-green-transportation-options-senior-citizens/. See also, *Kiplinger's Retirement Report*, "Getting Around When You No Longer Drive," November 2012, P.18.

67. Another option, but further out on the horizon: Daniel Fagnant and Kara Kockleman, "The Travel and Environmental Implications of Share Autonomous Vehicles, Using Agent-Based Model Scenarios," Transportation Research Board. January 2014.

68. the assumption that the average driver would be between 30 and 40 years of age: Larry Tibbits and Kim Lariviere, "The Future Highway Infrastructure- How it Can Help Older Drivers and Pedestrians Retain Their Mobility," in Coughlin and D'Ambrosio, *op. cit.* Chapter 6.

69. part of the expense may be the business process: for a discussion of this see two community articles. John Harris, "Taxi Medallions are a Terrible Idea," *The Brookline(Ma.) Tab*, Feb. 13, 2014, and Ignacio Laguarda, "Making the Cab System more Market Driven," *The Brookline Tab*, Feb. 20, 2014.

70. teens today are delaying getting a driver's license: Teens Delay Licensure: A Cause for Concern?" AAA Foundation Study, Aug. 1, 2013.

71. properties in the outer suburbs fell far more in value: Tanya Snyder, "CNT Busts 'Drive Till You Qualify' Myth in the DC Region," Streetsblog USA, January 21, 2013.

72. The goal is to calculate the full costs of housing plus transportation: See a useful tool from Center for Neighborhood Technology, http://abogo.cnt.org/. Another site from the same group: http://htindex.cnt.org/

Chapter Four: All Linked Up- Transportation, Homes, and Environment

73. With SAVS, there are likely to be less traffic accidents: Daniel Fagnant and Kara Kockelman, "Preparing a Nation for Autonomous Vehicles: Opportunities, Barriers and Policy Recommendations," Transportation Research Board, January 2014.

74. Forty five percent of those driving hybrid powered (models): Jim Gorzelany, "Electric-Car Buyers Younger and Richer than Hybrid Owners," *Forbes*. April 22, 2014.

75. Today, about four in ten homes: Mousumi Sarkar, "How American Homes Vary by the Year they were Built," U.S. Census Bureau. Working Paper No 2011-18.

76. A recent home that won awards: National Association of Home Builders, "Ted Clifton: Plan and Plan Again" http://www.nahb.org/generix/aspx?genericContentID=210215&fromGSA=1.

77. the rate of loss doubled from 20 to more than 40 percent: Arthur Nelson, "Leadership in a New Era," *Journal of the American Planning Association*, Autumn 2006, Vol. 72, No. 4.

78. convenience stores like 7-11: See, for example, a story by Mike Dunn, "Amazon Partners with 7-[aa]Eleven For In Store Pick Ups," *Digital Trends*, September 5, 2011.

79. When polled, they are more likely than Boomers: "Millennials in Adulthood," Pew Research Social and Demographic Trends. March 7, 2014.

80. A German researcher calculated carbon dioxide emissions: Eric Nabourney, "Why is Gaia Angy with Me," *The New York Times,* Feb 15, 2013. Note that there is no standardized methodology to calculate carbon footprints.

81. consumption dropped by 31 percent between 1978 and 2005: U.S. Energy Information Administration. Annual Energy Review 2009. Table 2.4.

82. Architects and builders shift toward a housing infrastructure: Brian Dumaine, "Houses that Flip and Fold," *Fortune.* June 19, 2013. See also news of a modular home-manufacturing business called Blu Homes. These homes are said to use half as much energy as similarly sized homes built with more typical techniques. www.bluhomes.com.

CHAPTER FIVE: BOOMER CASH OUT?

83. one of the most startling trends: Lori Trawinki, "Nightmare on Main Street: Older Americans and the Mortgage Market Crisis," AARP Public Policy Institute. 2012. Also see an article by Henry Cisneros, "The Financial Implications of an Aging America," Bipartisan Policy Center, July 29, 2014.

84. One pundit says this was rational consumption: John R. Talbott, *Contagion*, Wiley, 2009. Talbott says many senior citizens used their homes as a bank account to finance their consumption.

85. As of December 2011 an estimated 17 percent of older households: "Nearly Retired, Lugging a Mortgage," This is quoted from a research presentation by Olivia Mitchell and Annamaria Lusardi, The Center for Retirement Research at Boston College, September 24, 2013.

86. The AARP estimates that about 1.5 million people: Lori Trawinki, Nightmare on Main Street, *op. cit.*

87. a recent study found that Baby Boomers showed little inclination: "Are Aging Baby Boomers Abandoning the Single-Family Nests?" Fannie Mae Housing Insights, Volume 4, Issue 3. June 12, 2014.

88. The high cost of retirement may have been "oversold": Laurence Kotlikoff and Scott Burns, *The Clash of Generations: Saving Ourselves, our Kids, and Our Economy,* MIT Press, 2012.

89. the first generation to enter retirement: Amy Traub and Demos, "In the Red: Older Americans and Credit Card Debt," AARP Public Policy Institute. January, 2013.

90. New retirees may be surprised when they are turned down: Kenneth Harney, "Retirees May Find they don't Qualify to Refinance their Mortgages," *The Los Angeles Times,* May 27, 2012.

91. To qualify for a reverse mortgage: A useful overview can be found at various commercial sites such as www.reversemortgage.org and at a government site: portal.hud/gov/hudportal/HUD?src=/program_offices/housing /sfh/hecm/hecmhome. For an older valuable book with lots of practical advise- see Sarah Lyons and John Lucas, *Reverse Mortgages for Dummies,* Wiley Publishing. Hoboken, NJ. 2005. Since the book was published in 2005, the adverse things that "could never happen" are now evident.

92. The AARP and legal counselors have weighed in:
Carole Fleck, "Are Reverse Mortgages Helpful or Hazardous? "
AARP Bulletin, April. 2013.

93. The state government in Florida: Josh Salman "Florida
to Offer Reverse Mortgage Help," *The Sarasota Herald –
Tribune*, Nov. 12, 2013.

**94. The reverse mortgage has been described as an
empty balloon:** this example comes from
www.reversemortgage.org/About/FeaturesofReverseMortgages.
aspx. The site also has a useful reverse mortgage calculator.

95. In 2013 the US Congress: Andrew Miga, "FHA Needs
1.7B to Cover Reverse Mortgage Loss," *USA Today*, September
27, 2013.

**96. The Consumer Financial Protection Bureau has also
warned:** Carole Fleck, AARP. *op. cit.*

**97. In these models, the reverse mortgage is used as a
line of credit:** "Tap Home Equity When Markets Drop,"
Kiplinger's Retirement Report, November, 2012.

98. home equity represents 80%: The 80% is cited from the
2007 Survey of Consumer Finance by Stephanie Moulton. It is
summarized by Ashlea Ebeling, "A Troubling Housing Misstep
by Boomers," *Forbes*, March 19, 2012. Moulton is a public policy
professor and a former reverse mortgage counselor for AARP.

99. younger people are favoring urban locations: See
discussion by Jed Kolko, Chief Economist at Trulia. He notes
many demographic differences among this group and predicts
they will make choices very different from previous generations.
Kolko is cited by Lisa Prevost, "Home Loans for Millenials," *The
New York Times*, June 13, 2013.

100. Westchester and Suffolk, and Nassau have experienced declines: Joseph Berger, "Suburbs Try to Prevent an Exodus as Young Adults Move to Cities and Stay," *The New York Times*, April 16, 2014.

101. This group, which was not wealthy to begin: The State of the Nation's Housing, 2013. Joint Center for Housing Studies. Harvard University.

102. The National Association of Realtors: "NAR Survey of Generational Trends Shows Younger Buyers More Optimistic," NAR news releases. www.realtor.org. July 2013.

103. A demographic crossroad: Lee Gallagher, *The End of The suburbs: Where the American Dream is Moving*. Portfolio. 2013.

104. It is estimated that 20 to 30 percent: John Talbott. *The Coming Crash in the Housing Market: 10 things you can do now to protect your most valuable investment*. McGraw Hill 2003.

CHAPTER FIVE-PART TWO

105. the movoto site: movoto.com was searched in February, 2014. To replicate this search with current sizes and prices enter the city name at www.movoto.com/market-trends/.

106. these new homes have small lots but upscale amenities: Kate McLaughlin, Luxury Homes That Are Better, Not Bigger. *The Wall St. Journal*, February 6, 2014

107. www.seniorhomes.com. The fine print... how we make money: "We make money by helping senior housing providers find residents. Our featured listings are for providers with whom we have a commercial relationship"

108. Based on a 2012 study done by Rutgers: Emily Greenfield, Andrew Scharlach, Carrie Graham, Joan Davitt, and Amanda Lehning "A National Overview of Villages: Results from a 2012 Organizational Survey." Rutgers School of Social Work. December 1, 2012.

109. Karen Bush, Louise Machinist and Jean McQuillin. *My House, Our House: Living Far Better for Far Less in a Cooperative Household*. St. Lynn's Press. 2013.

110. Social historians estimate that between a third and half: Ruth Graham, "Boardinghouses: Where the city was born," *The Boston Globe*, January 13, 2013. 116.

111. There are also popular books on the topic: Jim Miller, "Resources for Seniors Interested in Retiring Abroad," *The Huffington Post*. February 3, 2013.

112. the attraction, according to Marketwatch, www.marketwatch.com/story/retire-here-not-there-costa-rica-2013-07-16

113. They add that bargains can be found. (www.aarp.org/home-garden/livable-communities/info-07-2010/best-places-retire-abroad-mexico-puerto-vallarta.html).

114. No one knows exactly how many people have opted: Kerry Hannon, "13 tips for a Working Retirement---Abroad," *Forbes*, September 20, 2013.

CHAPTER SIX: GRAY HOMES, SHRINKING THE KIDS

115. One early media critic called this: Neil Postman, *Amusing Ourselves to Death: Public Discourse in the Age of Show Business*, Penguin Books, 1985. The theme that something is amiss in the suburbs is also raised in an older book published in 2000, *Suburban Nation* by Adres Duany, Elizabeth Plater-Zyberk and Jeff Speck, Chapter 7.

116. So, middle-class parents: David Brooks, *On Paradise Drive: How We Live Now (And Always Have in the Future Tense)*, Simon and Schuster, 2005

117. a next generation of home-buyers shows: Lisa Prevost, "Home Loans for Millennials," *The New York Times*, June 13, 2013. The research is citing a study by the Urban Land Institute. About 60 percent of Millennials say they prefer a mix of housing choices. Down the road, 40 percent expect to live in some type of multifamily housing.

118. 45 percent of younger Baby Boomers, born between 1957 and 1964 had marriages: U.S. Bureau of Labor Statistics. TED: The Editor's Desk. November 8, 2013, http://www.bls.gov/opub/ted_20131108.htm

119. The delinquency among student borrowers increased: "Proliferation in Student Debt Driven by Weakest Borrowers, Fed Finds," February 14, 2014. *The Wall St. Journal.* The student debt rose 12% to $1.08 trillion in 2013 according to the Federal Reserve Bank of New York. It is the second largest form of household credit, after mortgages.

120. if there's supposed to be a stigma: Kim Parker, Pew Research Center, The Boomerang Generation, Feeling OK About Living with Mom and Dad," Pew Social Trends. 2012.

121. In the 2011 Current Population Study: "More Young Adults are Living in Their Parent's Home, Census Bureau Reports," U.S. Census Bureau. Newsroom. Nov. 3, 2011.

122. Multigenerational family household: *"Sharing a household with family members is a time-honored strategy for stretching thin resources,"* this quote is cited in a paper by Laryssa Mykyta "Economic Downturns and the Failure-to-Launch: The Living Arrangements of Young Adults in the US 1995-2011," SEHSD Working Paper 2012-24. U.S. Census Bureau. She cites a 2009 Pew Study called "Home for the Holidays...and every other day." http://www.pewsocialtrends/org/assets/pdf/home-for-the-holidays.pdf. See also, Suzanne Macartney and Laryssa Mykyta, "Poverty and Shared Households by State: 2011," U.S. Census Bureau, ACS Survey Briefs, Nov. 2012. Also, "In Post-Recession Era, Young Adults Drive Continuing Rise in MultiGenerational Living," Pew Social and Demographic Trends. July 17, 2014. www.pewsocialtrends.org/

123. Gallup (poll) estimates that 29 percent of adults under age 35: www.gallup.com/poll/167426/aged-living-parents.aspx. (2/13/2014).

124. A Pew Study estimates: Richard Fry, "Millennials still lag in forming their own households," Pew Research Center, Factank. October 18, 2013.

125. The parent child bond rarely runs as strongly: This quote is attributable to Hendrik Hartog. In Brian Bethune, "The Curse of Small Families," *Macleans*, September 3, 2013.

126. Joel Kotkin: *The Next Hundred Million: America in 2050.* Penguin Books. 2011. Kotkin is bullish on the suburbs, and anticipates that a new large immigrant population will choose to live there. In an interview with the blog *Grist* (3/30/12) he notes that urban life does not necessarily mean a high density lifestyle. He cites areas that blend urban living and single-family detached homes, like Staten Island, Queens, and the San Fernando Valley (Ca).

127. High poverty suburban communities. See Ian Berube, "The State of Metropolitan America: Suburbs and the 2010 Census," Brookings Institute. July 14, 2011.

Chapter Seven: The Game Changer–Boomers and Technology

128. After World War II Americans Started Producing Larger Families: there is a qualification– It would be more accurate to say that Americans started producing replacement families. The birth rate had been unusually low, due to the Great Depression and World War II.

129. Boomers lined up at motor vehicle departments to get their licenses: http://www.fhwa.dot.gov/policyinformation/statistics/2010/dv1c.cfm. In 1972 there were 118 million drivers and 119 million registered vehicles. The next year it had grown to 122 million drivers and 126 million vehicles. As of 2010, there were 210 million registered drivers and 242 registered vehicles.

130."disruptive technology": See an article by Caroline Howard, "Disruption vs. Innovation. What is the Difference? " *Forbes*, March 27, 2013.

131. The U.S. government has a program that replaces old, substandard homes: http://portal.hud.gov-hudportal/HU?ssrc-hudprograms/home-program

132. This period was called the Gilded Age: For a scenic introduction to the gilded age and "the cottages" of Newport,

Rhode Island history begin at
http://www.newportmangions.org.

133. Not surprisingly, the market for these properties dropped: "A New Gilded Age for Newport? Mansions in Demand." CNBC, Sept. 16, 2013. Larry Ellison purchased a Newport home. Also, the third highest purchase price in the town's history took place in 2013 at $14 million.

134. The company was sold for 8 billion in stock: Martin Peers and Shalini Ramachandran, "Bye Bye for Blockbuster," *The Wall St. Journal*, Nov. 7, 2013. Ironically, RedBox, which rents DVDs through vending machines brings yet another technological upheaval to the video business.

135. Older housing stock is highly desirable in these cities: Edward Glaeser, *Triumph of the City: How Our Greatest Invention Makes Us Richer, Smarter, Greener, Healthier and Happier*. Penguin Books, 2011.

136. Now these spaces are showing their age as tastes and technology march on: For an insightful analysis of how amenities in homes change see Mousumi Sarkar, "How American Homes Vary by the Year They Were Built," Working Paper No. 2011-8. U.S. Census Bureau. June 2011. For example, about 22 percent of homes have a family/great room and 80 percent have a garage. Before 1960, only 12.7 percent of homes had family/great rooms and only 60 percent had garages.

137. This cohort, sometimes called Digital Natives: The term Digital Native is attributed to Mark Prensky, On the Horizon. MCB University Press, Vol. 9 No. 5, October 2001. Source: www.wikipedia.com. Clearly not all young people born after 1990 are conversant with new technology, and others, born earlier, are totally fluent. The term is a metaphor for those most comfortable and at-home with the latest development in computer technology and the Internet.

138. Not only have the video stores closed: Barbara Farfan, "2014 Retail Stores Closing, Going Out of Business, Filing Bankruptcy. All 2013 Store Closings," *U.S. Retail Industry* http://retailindustry.about.com/od/USRetailStoreClosingInfoFA Qs/fl/All-2014-Store-Closings-US-Retail-Industry-Chains-to-Close-Stores_2.htm

139. Once I started traveling and hiking a lot: David Coleman, "Robert Rhinehart: Dreaming of the Skies and Traveling Light," *The New York Times*, November 8, 2013.

140. Today, most auction houses would refuse the items: P4A Antiques Reference (available at most public libraries). Also, discussion by author with Peter Jones, curator of English antiquities for Bonhams, Los Angeles. May, 2013.

141. The industry estimates that one in six Americans use off-site storage: Self Storage Association Fact Sheet. http://www.selfstorage.org/ssa/content/navigationmenu/aboutssa/factsheet/

142. Ikea has seen this opportunity and is marketing directly to the next generation: Barbara Thau, "Home Retailers Target Millennial," *HFN Home Furnishing News.* Sept. 2013. Millennials are predicted to outnumber the Baby Boomers in sheer size and buying power by 2020.

143. It is known as the Share Economy: National Public Radio Special Series. "The Sharing Economy: A Shift Away from Ownership?" http://www.npr.org/series/244583579/the-sharing-economy-a-shift-away-from-ownership. See also, Ruth Bender, "For Rent: Trendy Jeans, Cars, Appliances," *The Wall St. Journal*, Dec. 2, 2013.

144. Today there are an estimated 800,000 car sharing members: Susan Shaheen, and Adam Cohen, "Innovative Mobility Carsharing Outlook: Carsharing Market Overview,

Analysis and Trends," University of California Berkeley, Transportation Sustainability Research Center. 2013.

145. the average car is parked and idle for 95% of the day: Donald Shoup, **The High Cost of Free Parking**, APA Planners Press, 2011. The 95% number is derived from the 1995 Nationwide Personal Transportation Survey (NPTS). The average time drivers spent in the car was 73 minutes (1.2 hours). Assuming one car per driver, this gives 5% as the time each car is in motion.

146. The sales growth of pet products slowed but they still went up: Andrew Martin, "For the Dogs Has a Whole New Meaning," *The New York Times,* June 4, 2011.

147. According to a recent real estate survey of 1000 adults: Millennials Wouldn't Buy Their Parents' Home," *Realty Times*, May 31, 2013. A related piece is by James Briggs in the *Baltimore Business Journal*, June 13, 2013 called, "Letter from a Millennial: We're not going to buy your house."

148. one of the more novel amenities... http://selfservedogwashbusiness.com/self-serve-dog-washes-are-latest-trend-at-the-car-wash-show/ March 2014.

149. A 2013 inquiry by a California Congressman has found that the dynamics of house buying have: Trey Garrison, "California Congressman goes on REO-to-Rental Warpath," *Housing Wire*. March 6, 2014. The Congressman is Mark Takano, a Democrat from California.

150. giant institutional investors: David Dayen, "Your New Landlord Works on Wall Street," *The New Republic*, Feb 12, 2013.

151. A real estate professor at George Mason: this quote is from Anthony Sanders, a professor of real estate. It is cited by

Akane Otani, "Big Spenders: Retail Sales Report Mirrors Millennials Buying Habits," *Christian Science Monitor.* Oct. 29, 2013.

152. Emily Badger, "The Anxiety of the Forever Renter," *The Atlantic Cities.* November 14, 2011.

153. the large pizza chains and franchises are gaining share: Julie Jargon, "Apps are Wrecking Mom-and-Pop Pizza Shops," *The Wall St. Journal,* Feb. 7, 2014.

154. Have a good day exchanged between virtual strangers: Sherry Turkle, *Alone Together.* Basic Books, 2011. This book makes a compelling case of how we expect more from technology and less from each other.

155. Teens are getting their driver's licenses later: Jerry Hirsch, "Who Needs a Car? Smartphones are driving teens Social Lives," March 15, 2013, *The Los Angeles Times.* Driving once allowed teens, "...to go where you want, do what you want, see who you want and, in some sense, be who you want...The Internet has made the freedom that comes with a license anticlimactic." Drivers ages 15 to 20 accounted for 3.4% of new-car sales in 1985, or about 500,000 vehicles, according to CNW Research, an automotive market research firm. That dropped to 2% last year, or just 300,000 vehicles. Many of today's teenagers won't form the same emotional attachment to driving as their parents, who aspired to luxury or performance cars as status symbol.

156. one of the paradoxes of new technology: Edward Glaeser, *The Triumph of the City, op. cit.* This is called Jevon's Complementary Corollary. Jevon's paradox refers to a situation in which efficiency improvements lead to more, not less, consumption. The nineteenth-century English economist William Stanley Jevons noted that more fuel-efficient steam engines did not lead to less coal consumption. Better engines made energy use less expensive, and helped move the world to an industrial era powered by coal.

157. long commutes stretch our friendships: Charles Montgomery, *Happy City*, Farrar, Straus and Giroux, 2013.

158. The closer you are to cafes and movie theaters.... This quote is from Marianne Cusato with Daniel DiClerico, *The Just Right Home: Buying, Renting, Moving- Or Just Dreaming- Find Your perfect Match!* Workman Publishing, 2012. It is cited in Gallagher, *op. cit.*

159. instead, they predict new demand for attached units: "America in 2013:Key Findings on Housing, Community, Transportation and the Generations," Urban Land Institute. www.uli.org

CONCLUSIONS AND RECOMMENDATIONS

160. the number of (two-adult) households: Nancy McGuckin and Jana Lynott, *op. cit.*

161. one-in-six jobs in the U.S.: "Transportation and The Economy" Transportation Energy Data Book, Oak Ridge National Laboratory. Table 10.17. http://cta.ornl.gov/data/chapter10.shtml

162. younger workers are able to keep their employment options flexible: Center for Neighborhood Technology, *op. cit.*

163. Some observers think that there will be a release of 26 million homes by 2030: The Bipartisan Policy Center estimates there will be 11.3 million homes in this decade and up to 15 million more between 2020 and 2030. See, "Demographic Challenges and Opportunities for U.S. Housing Market," March

2012. Professor Arthur Nelson from the University of Utah is a demographer and has predicted a larger glut of conventional-lot, single-family homes.

164. part of the debt problem...is that families converted: John Talbott, *Contagion: The Financial Epidemic That is Sweeping the Global Economy*,Wiley, 2008.

165. the best lawyer cannot keep the property: For a useful discussion see "Reverse Mortgages and Your Heirs," *Kiplinger's Retirement Report*, March, 2014.

166. Women stop driving sooner than men: Sandra Rosenbloom,"The Travel and Mobility Needs of Older People Now and in the Future," in Coughlin and D'Ambrosio, *op. cit.*

167. Whether Baby Boomers will do so (self regulate driving) is unknown: Joseph Coughlin and Steven Proulx, "If Demographics is Destiny, Are We Preparing for It..." In Coughlin and D'Ambrosio, *op. cit.*

168. It turns out that trips for medical visits: Nancy McGuckin and Jana Lynott *op. cit.* The authors pose whether changes in the delivery of medical care have increased the amount of time spent traveling to medical appointments.

169. Eight in ten of these were women: Barbara Lipman, Jeffrey Lubell, and Emily Salomon, "Housing an Aging Population, Are we prepared?" Center for Housing Policy, 2012. According to their 2008 data, only 42% of women age 65 and older live with a spouse, compared with 72% of men that age. Among those no longer married, 50% of the women live alone, 17% with other relatives and 2% with non-relatives.

170. According to U.S. News the ten (best) places to go carless: Emily Brandon, "10 Places to Go Carless in

Retirement," *U.S. News*, March 21, 2011. See also, "Where are Boomers headed? Not Back to the City," *Forbes*, Oct. 17, 2013.

171. The community values professed: Brand decided that his early stance of emphasizing individualism should be replaced with one favoring community. From en.wikipedia.org/wiki/Whole-earth-catalog

172. people run back into their burning homes: John Talbott, op. cit.

173. there was a single group: www.beaconhillvillage.org

ABOUT THE AUTHOR

Jane Gould is a Baby Boomer, born in 1954. Since growing up, something Baby Boomers are reluctant to acknowledge, she has lived in six different 'old' homes and owned about eleven cars, some old, some new. Her first car was a 1970 Plymouth Valiant convertible, which she drove to high school.

Dr. Gould holds a PhD from the University of Pennsylvania and a Master's Degree from Cornell University, both in the communications field. Since 1993 she has worked with on large transportation projects, beginning with a feasibility study of electric vehicles for the state of California. She has taught and done research at the University of California Institute of Transportation Studies (Irvine), The London Business School (London, U.K.) and at UCLA (Los Angeles). At UCLA she worked in Transportation on sustainability, public transportation, and new technologies. She has published extensively in the transportation field, and specializes in transportation surveys. She currently manages a real-estate portfolio and divides her time between San Francisco and Boston.

You can follow her blog at http://agingin suburbia.com and on twitter at @janegould_PhD.

Made in the USA
Lexington, KY
31 August 2015